Creating Educational Justice

Creating Educational Justice

Learning from Black Home Educators

CHERYL FIELDS-SMITH

HARVARD EDUCATION PRESS
CAMBRIDGE, MASSACHUSETTS

Paperback ISBN 9781682539682

Library of Congress Cataloging-in-Publication Data

Names: Fields-Smith, Cheryl, author.
Title: Creating educational justice : learning from Black home educators / Cheryl Fields-Smith.
Description: Cambridge, Massachusetts : Harvard Education Press, [2025] | Includes bibliographical references and index.
Identifiers: LCCN 2024052973 | ISBN 9781682539682 (paperback)
Subjects: LCSH: Children, Black—Education—United States. | Home schooling—United States. | Educational equalization—United States.
Classification: LCC LC2743 .F54 2025 | DDC 371.04/208996073—dc23/eng/20250108
LC record available at https://lccn.loc.gov/2024052973

Published by Harvard Education Press,
an imprint of the Harvard Education Publishing Group

Harvard Education Press
8 Story Street
Cambridge, MA 02138

Cover Design: Jackie Shepherd Design
Cover Image: The img (laptop), fishStok (pie charts), Sensvector (man), IgorMass (woman), ProximaCentauri1 (girl) and Dedraw Studio (background pattern), all via Shutterstock

The typefaces in this book are Adobe Garamond Pro and Myriad Pro.

Creating Educational Justice: Learning from Black Home Educators is dedicated to brave Black parents who break from the "status quo" when it comes to the education of their children and forge new ways of engaging in the teaching and learning process on behalf of Black children. May your journey ultimately enhance learning experiences for all children within and outside traditional schools.

Contents

CONTENTS

Introduction

Imagine it is 2006. You are Mrs. Robinson, and that momentous time when you must send your precious little one, Veronica, to a formal educational institution for the first time is approaching. Your state laws mandate that five-year-old children must attend a kindergarten program of the parents' choosing, and you must now inform the state of your decision. You have watched Veronica grow and thrive under your care, and your deepest desire is that she will continue to do so in school. With due diligence, you and your spouse have reviewed every option available to you in your huge, racially segregated urban school district. Each of you attended public schools and completed a graduate-level education. Conversely, both of you have also observed the consequences of not having a good education; none of your siblings and now none of your siblings' children have completed high school.

Moreover, through your research, you have learned that your resegregated, locally assigned public school, which is within walking distance of your home, has a poor achievement record compared with the elementary schools in the northern, predominantly White portion of the school district. Your assigned public school also has fewer resources, such as limited music education, no foreign language education, and a lack of enrichment programming, compared with schools on the northern side of your district. Even though the school district you live in has numerous charter schools and magnet schools, attendance policies require families to live in proximity to those options to attend, and unfortunately, you live on the wrong side of those boundaries. There are no other public school options available for your child because of where you live. You found a private Montessori school, but it is too far north in the school district to qualify for district-provided transportation, which means you would have to provide your own, a trip that could take up to an hour of travel time each way. Moving to the northern section of the school district, where more—and better—schooling options exist, is out of the question because, though you are doing relatively well financially, the homes on that side of the district cost much more than you can afford. The only remaining option is homeschooling, but Mr. Robinson is dead set against it—he has a deep commitment to public education because his predominantly Black public school education provided him with a mostly positive learning experience.

Where would you want to send little Veronica for her kindergarten experience if you were Mrs. Robinson? Why?

Recounting the challenging decision to send Veronica to the locally assigned public school, the real Mrs. Robinson shared that she and her husband had hoped kindergarten would provide a gentle introduction to school. "But what we found out was that the school system saw kindergarten as . . . kind of pre–first grade. So when they go in, they're expected to sit down, be quiet, and do their work. It's not so much play—you know, interactive learning play. It's not really focused on that." Mr. Robinson added, "And the testing thing. . . . They were doing that on the first day!"

School staff's responses to Mr. and Mrs. Robinson's questions raised additional concerns. Mr. Robinson shared that during an open house before the school year started, he asked the principal,

> "Why do you have twenty-two new teachers this year?"
>
> And she said, "Well, change is good."
>
> I said, "I've done some work," and I didn't try to present myself as a person who's dealt with these kinds of issues in my profession, but I said, "Well, from what I know, stability is important. It's important for the education of poor Black children. It's important for the Black children out here."
>
> And she said, "Well, I think change is good."

Mr. Robinson perceived this response as dismissive of his concerns. Later, after dropping their daughter off for the first time, the Robinsons lingered a bit to get the feel of the school and to make sure their child would be all right. As they were lingering, they bumped into the assistant principal, who had Veronica by the hand as they were walking in the hallway.

Mr. Robinson reported, "The assistant principal had taken [Veronica] out of the classroom because she could see that she was having a hard time adjusting. So she was allowing [Veronica] to walk around the school with her to pass out papers to teachers. And when she made it back to the lobby, we, the parents, were still standing in the lobby, and then she was like, 'Parents! Are you still here?' And she said to me, 'Daddy, we can handle it,' in a condescending tone."

Mr. Robinson continued by sharing what would have worked for them: "This is what they could have done for us. If they had said, '[Mr. and Mrs. Robinson] you can sit in the classroom. Help her make the transition.' And that's the issue. Because you must reassure children. The first thing they didn't do—they didn't community build. I mean, this is kindergarten! She's only five years old. And she [the assistant principal] called me daddy! . . . I guess it was coming across as we're being overprotective."

After their daughter attended two and a half days of kindergarten in their locally assigned school, Mr. and Mrs. Robinson decided to educate her at home. They also later decided to homeschool their second child, who never experienced public schools at all.

The Robinsons' decision to homeschool after only two days of interaction within their locally assigned school may appear drastic and rash. Other parents may have chosen to accept the situation with the hope that things would improve as their child continued to transition into the classroom setting. However, the Robinsons' interaction with school staff could also be perceived as the beginning of a parent-school relationship in which parents were marginalized or even disenfranchised from engaging in their children's education in the school. The Robinsons did not want to accept the conditions they experienced in these first two days, which, rather than building trust, included belittlement of the Robinsons' engagement in and care for their daughter's education. They chose home education to retain their ability to have a say in their child's education and to ensure she had the best learning context possible.

Like the Robinsons seventeen years ago, Black families today are increasingly choosing home education for their children. Recent headlines have touted the "rise of Black homeschooling," referencing a 2021 Census Bureau report that documented an increase from approximately 3 percent to 16 percent in home education among Black families from April 2020 to October 2020.[1] This surge in Black home education may have been prompted by the COVID-19 pandemic shutdown, which led to a sudden shift to online learning and thus provided parents with a fuller view of their children's learning context. Many did not like what they observed. With everyone home, parents had the opportunity to become more aware of, and engaged, in their children's education.

However, focusing only on the postpandemic surge obscures the fact that Black home education had been steadily increasing before the pandemic, as suggested by earlier reports.[2] In fact, data from a 2006 study of Black home education informed the opening vignette.[3] The Robinson family's experience demonstrates a few of the key findings across forty-six Black homeschool families' decision-making regarding school choice. The Robinson vignette demonstrates that the decision to homeschool does not come easily to some Black families. Indeed, this family wanted their local assigned public school to work for their children. However, the sociopolitical context, including the legal resegregation of public schools and boundaries placed on access to school choice options, contributed to the Robinsons' decision to homeschool. Additionally, the school administration's disregard of the Robinsons' desire to be engaged in their child's education also contributed to their decision to homeschool. Mr. and Mrs. Robinson's own school experiences (positive and negative) also informed their decision to pursue home education. In this vignette, we see the multiple layers and complexity of a family's decision to homeschool.

Black home education research draws on the rich educational history of African Americans to deepen the understanding of ongoing Black educational challenges beyond the reported statistics. On the surface, it may seem that the increased prevalence of homeschooling among Black families signals a rejection of the ideals of desegregation and public education, but the research shows this is a false narrative.[4] As will be elaborated later in this chapter, African Americans have always had to teach themselves. Rather than a departure from our educational history, the Black home education movement of today represents a continuation of our legacy of self-agency and self-determination in the pursuit of education. Further, Black home education research corroborates and provides humanized insights to the many problems that plague Black education in public schools, such as lack of access to gifted education, disproportionality in the use of discipline, marginalization of Black parents' engagement, and overrepresentation of Black students in special education. Black home education research documents the emotional toil Black parents and children experience as they navigate racialized experiences in traditional schools, both public and private.[5]

Creating Educational Justice foregrounds the perspectives of sixty-three Black home educators who participated in three different research studies conducted between 2006 and 2021. Together, the Black families represent diverse perspectives in approaches to Black home education (e.g., unschooling, multicultural learning, African-centered learning), demographic diversity among Black home education families (e.g., family structure; rural, suburban, or urban location; socioeconomic status), and varying motivations to home educate. Chapter 1 provides an overview of the diversity among the sixty-three home educators whose experiences and voices inspired this book.

As it was for the Robinsons, homeschooling was the second choice for how most Black parents (forty-nine out of the sixty-three families) wanted their children to be educated. They decided to homeschool after first choosing to enroll their children in traditional schools (public or private). These parents perceived that remaining in those schools would be destructive to their children's academic progress, detrimental to their children's positive racial identity, or dangerous to their children's overall well-being. For the remaining eleven Black families, their decisions to homeschool from birth were influenced by personal parenting beliefs and negative perceptions of their locally assigned public schools fueled by media and performance statistics.

Whether Black parents decided to homeschool from birth or after enrolling their children in traditional schools, they expressed empathy for the staff and administration of public schools and offered constructive criticism.[6] Black home educators understood the pressures public school teachers faced with large class sizes, overemphasis on test scores, and a rigid curriculum. Most Black home educators in this study did not have an adversarial relationship with public education; quite the opposite. They instead offered traditional schools feedback grounded in a desire for "them [schools] to do better." This is the spirit in which *Creating Educational Justice* is written. In this way, research on Black home education serves as a bridge between Black families and schools. By examining best practices in Black education, this research informs effective school reform on behalf of all children because it leads to advanced understanding of inclusive pedagogy, collaboration with all types of parents, increased awareness of personal bias, and the promotion of students' empowerment in their learning.

Additionally, we must consider that traditional schools have been plagued by a lingering educational opportunity gap for decades, which home education often enables families to overcome. How long should Black parents and children wait to gain access to schools that will serve them best? Unlike achievement measures, educational opportunities emphasize the social inequities and disparities that disadvantage some groups of students while advantaging others.[7] One opportunity gap Black children experience is the disenfranchisement of their parents from engagement and advocacy on behalf of their children within schools. Research has documented the marginalization of Black parents, including middle-class Black families, as they attempt to engage in their children's education.[8] Given their challenges in advocating on behalf of their children, it is no wonder that parents would choose home education.

Home education research has much to offer traditional schools pedagogically. At one time, homeschooling entailed a parent teaching their children at the kitchen table, a practice that likely would have been too idiosyncratic to inform traditional schools. But today, homeschooled children learn in a variety of settings, including classroom spaces with other homeschooled children, both in person and online. Additionally, research using a variety of methods has repeatedly indicated that homeschooled students perform as well as, or better than, their traditionally schooled peers.[9] Though the methodology used for such achievement comparisons has been critiqued, the point here is that different types of research methods, over a significant period of time, have consistently documented homeschooled students—including Black homeschooled students—achieving at the same level as, or higher than, their traditionally schooled counterparts.[10]

The purpose of this book is to center the voices of Black home educators in order to provide constructive feedback regarding what works for Black children, and ultimately all children. *Creating Educational Justice* advances the premise that if we want to know how to effectively educate Black children, we need to ask Black parents, particularly those who have chosen to assume full responsibility for their children's education through homeschooling. The insight Black home educators offer addresses controversial topics in education today, such as questions of pedagogy and theoretical perspectives on education. The next section provides an overview of existing Black home education literature and related theoretical frameworks, which have partially informed the definition of *educational justice* applied throughout this book.

REVIEW OF BLACK HOMESCHOOL RESEARCH AND ASSOCIATED THEORETICAL FRAMEWORKS

Research on Black home education has not entirely kept pace with the rise in the Black homeschool population. The available empirically based, published literature has evolved but remains relatively limited. Overall, the articles and books focused on Black home education have tended to use qualitative methods and placed an emphasis on Black parents' motivations to educate their children at home. Between 2010 and 2022, there was a proliferation of dissertations focused on Black homeschooling; however, these have been excluded from this review in order to focus on published work. In this section, I discuss research literature published from 2009, which is when the first empirically based article to focus exclusively on Black home education was published, through 2022. The literature is examined along with the evolution of theoretical and conceptual frameworks applied in the research.

Using a Parental Engagement Lens

At the outset, my colleague Meca Williams-Johnson and I conceptualized the phenomenon of homeschooling among Black families as "extreme parental engagement," meaning homeschooling represents the greatest and final point on a continuum of degrees to which parents can be engaged in their children's learning.[11] Blending concepts such as parental role construction with Urie Bronfenbrenner's ecological model and with Jane Van Galen's early homeschool categories (pedagogues and ideologues), we conceptualized Black homeschooling as parents' intense engagement in their children's learning, which occurs across multiple spaces within and beyond the home.[12] Black parents decide to engage in homeschooling based on a belief that they can make a difference in their children's education (parental role construction or parental self-efficacy) and on their own parenting experiences.

While Williams-Johnson and I found that elements of Black home educators' beliefs aligned with the pedagogue and idealogue categories established by Van Galen's work, our findings also revealed a new category of ethnological factors that motivated Black parents' decisions to homeschool.[13] Specifically, seventeen out of the twenty-four participating Black home educators described pedagogue-like beliefs related to their decisions to homeschool, meaning they disagreed with the instructional approaches their children experienced in public or private schools. These parents made the decision to homeschool as early as kindergarten and as late as high school. In addition, seven of the twenty-four Black home educators expressed idealogue beliefs when describing their motivations to home educate, which represented a deep belief that parents, not an institution, should be children's first teachers. Notably, these seven parents made the decision to homeschool from birth. The majority (nineteen of twenty-four) of the parents described experiences within their children's schools (public and private) that were steeped in issues surrounding race, anti-Blackness, and negative interactions with the school, which also contributed to their decisions to educate at home.

Black home educators perceived diverse ways in which racialized experiences within schools informed their decisions to homeschool. Parents reported concerns with processes used to attempt to identify their children for special-needs services, particularly when such perceived needs were conflated with behavior issues. Additionally, Black parents coupled their concerns with the sociocultural context of racism overall and their own experiences with racism, particularly for their sons. Parents held negative perceptions of teachers' and schools' expectations overall. For example, a parent shared, "In school, children of color tend not to be expected to excel."[14] This study found that home education provided Black children refuge from intentional and subtle experiences with racism that could harm their racial identity.

However, the existing parental involvement frameworks did not fully explain the phenomenon of Black parents deciding to educate their children at home. For example, theories about how parents decide to be involved in their children's education ignored the role of emotions in influencing those decisions.[15] Indeed, because home education was a second choice, many Black parents only decided to homeschool after they had attempted to engage in advocacy within traditional schools to resolve issues such as children being labeled behavior problems, pedagogical issues in meeting their children's learning needs, or similar intense situations. Additionally, parental involvement frameworks and theories tend to ignore how the cultural historical context of engagement varies from one racial or ethnic group to another within schools. Therefore, a more culturally responsive framework for Black home education would better serve this research.

Culturally Responsive Conceptual Frameworks: African-Centered Lens and Resistance

In 2012 and 2013, two publications emerged that conceptualized Black home education, one from an Afrocentric lens and the other as a form of resistance.[16] The first detailed a study of seventy-four Black home educators that applied an African-centered lens. It found that Black parents' decisions to homeschool stemmed from the need to protect their children from racism or racialized experiences within schools, and it identified Black home educators as "racial protectionists." This study further documented the ways in which homeschooling provided Black children the freedom to explore their racial identity and self-esteem.

Similarly, the second study conceptualized Black home education as a form of resistance based on bell hooks's essay "Homeplace."[17] In the essay, hooks describes how Black women/mothers were empowered inside their homes during the Jim Crow era. The term *homeplace* refers to the ways Black women/mothers historically used everyday actions within their homes to shield and edify their children during segregation so they could resist, endure, and overcome the undue hate, racism, and oppression they faced outside their homes daily. The unseen intentional actions taken within Black families' homes provided the necessary relief, restoration, and realignment to counter the undeserved treatment Black children experienced daily outside their homes.

Likewise, the authors of the 2013 publication conceptualized today's Black homeschool movement as a contemporary reclaiming and reprioritizing of "homeplace."[18] Black families in Metro Atlanta and Metro DC reported similar motivations to homeschool in response to negative experiences within their children's schools, including teachers' low expectations of their children's potential, children being labeled as behavior problems, and issues surrounding their children's safety. Black parents who chose to educate their children at home were no longer accepting the status quo when it came to their children's education. According to the authors of the 2013 publication, "It could be argued that today, black homeschooling mothers are 'flipping-the-script' on their previously ascribed roles as 'domestic-other' and 'working-mother' and they are instead powerfully reclaiming domesticity as their personal choice and individual right."[19] By homeschooling today, Black families create the necessary educational spaces to ensure their children's academic success along with their positive racial identity in ways that are not always available within traditional schools.

Furthermore, research focused on single Black mothers who homeschooled their children expanded the concept of Black home education as resistance by grounding the work in elements of African American resistance theory, Black feminist thought (BFT), and endarkened feminist epistemology (EFE).[20] A thorough examination of the history of Black education in the US revealed numerous ways in which Black communities have had to resist to obtain quality education for their children.[21] Here, *resistance* specifically refers to African American resistance theory, the action of pursuing change from outside traditional systems in response to being denied access to educational opportunities within the system.[22] Historically, and today, African American resistance can be public or private, collective, or individual, and it can be directed internally or externally. Today's Black home education movement represents resistance against a seemingly less overt, somewhat intangible force compared with the oppression of the institution of slavery or Jim Crow laws, but the force is nonetheless destructive to our children.

CONTEMPORARY FRAMEWORKS

BFT and EFE—derived from Black women's ways of knowing and being—conceptually and methodologically ground this research on Black home education. The sixty-three Black families who participated in the research for this book were represented primarily by mothers. (Only two fathers participated in interviews with their wives, and one other divorced father represented his family by participating in an interview. None of the fathers engaged in focus groups or Sister Circles.) Therefore, mothers served as the primary educators for all of the families represented in this research.

Black Feminist Thought

BFT is not new; as the Combahee River Collective acknowledged decades ago, "Contemporary Black feminism is the outgrowth of countless generations of personal sacrifice, militancy, and work by our mothers and sisters."[23] Patricia Hill Collins's seminal work explained that while all Black women experience an intersection of oppressions based on race, gender, and class, we respond to them, and resist, in diverse ways.[24] This tenet enables us to understand that Black women are not a monolith. Therefore, rather than only seeking commonalities, researchers should be compelled to aim to understand the many ways in which Black women resist anti-Blackness and other forms of oppression in their lives. This is not to suggest that Black women cannot be a collective. Black women/mothers can indeed be bonded in a sisterhood, in our humanity, and in the struggle that permeates our daily lives, even with our uniqueness. The diversity among Black mothers' motivations, beliefs, and practices represents, in part, varied responses to the oppressions they or their children experienced within and outside traditional schools, as well as their perceptions of oppressions they experience.

BFT empowers Black women to engage in self-naming. As Black mothers identify as homeschoolers, they are in effect engaging in self-naming because they are identifying with a label that contemporarily has not been associated with the Black community. As they have done with other sociopolitically created labels, Black mothers have co-opted the term and made new meaning of it. Indeed, some Black mothers referred to themselves as home educators even when the state they lived in would not have counted their children among homeschoolers because they had enrolled in a public online charter school or some other government-run program. Black home educators did not define home education or homeschooling in terms of curriculum or program, but instead assigned themselves the home educator identity because they had assumed full responsibility for their children's education even if public education contributed a portion of their children's learning context. They self-identified as home educators because they did not give any other entity, even public schools, full control of the decision-making regarding their children's education. For the small number of Black home educators who chose to enroll their children in an online public charter school, this accounted for only a portion of their children's learning experiences. They also participated as members in homeschool co-ops, field trips, support groups, and other homeschool family interactions. Therefore, Black home educators, including those whose children attended public virtual charter schools, curated a variety of learning opportunities that enriched their children's interests, learning, and positive racial identities.

Overall, BFT empowers us as researchers to center the everyday practices of Black women/mothers as a form of activism and resistance to the oppression we experience daily, within and outside traditional schools. Black mothers who assume the role of home educator have chosen not to rely solely on conventional schooling as their own parents may have. These decisions come with personal and family sacrifices, but they choose home education with the hope and promise of providing their children with an education that will uplift their cultural and racial identities while also providing the flexibility and access to educational opportunities that enable their children to reach their full potential. Lingering systemic and individual anti-Black oppressions, within and outside schools, make necessary the use of BFT and similar theories developed for us and by us.

Endarkened Feminist Epistemology

Cynthia Dillard's EFE invites Black scholars, and other scholars of color, to reflect on cultural ancestry, cultural ways of being, and spirituality as critical functions of the research process. She reminds us that community consensus determines what counts as something worth knowing.[25] For the purposes of this book, I am featuring Black home educators as a community of themselves. This is important because even though they are quite diverse, they create and exist within their endarkened realities and communities in different ways from Black parents in conventional schools, as well as from other groups of people who also choose to home educate.

From my initial reading of EFE to numerous subsequent readings, I have felt seen, understood, and highly empowered as a researcher in ways that other frameworks such as social/cultural capital or parental role construction have never provided. EFE assumes that research serves as an intellectual and spiritual endeavor.[26] The link to spirituality aligns with how I was taught to approach qualitative research and what I observed from my doctoral program mentors, Vanessa Siddle Walker and Jackie Jordan Irvine, both of whom are African American female scholars. As EFE posits, I was taught that my research should be reciprocal, meaning that I should contribute to the communities in which I do my research rather than just collecting data and leaving. My researcher upbringing included learning to build genuine rapport with the parents I met as part of the research process. This takes time, but it is a critical part of gaining the trust of those with whom you do research. Further, EFE and my doctoral training espoused that it is the onus of each researcher to remain accountable to the communities in which we situate our work. Integrating the fundamental assumptions of EFE into this work resulted in culturally responsive methods that aligned with Black home educator mothers' ways of being as well.

DEFINING EDUCATIONAL JUSTICE

As BFT and EFE would support, the definition of educational justice that frames this book stems directly from the perspective of Black home educators and, more specifically, seminal findings in the application of child privacy law to Black homeschooling, which was conducted by legal scholar Najarian Peters.[27] Over the years, precedents established in child privacy law have supported individuals' rights to human dignity, individuality, peace of mind, freedom from future harm, self-determination, and even "the right to be left alone."[28] Yet, in her review, Peters found that these aspects of child privacy law had not been applied to the lives of Black people consistently. She explains,

> Black people's experience with the right to privacy has been inconsistent at best. Black children are disproportionately denied the experience and attendant benefits of child privacy. Foregrounding the essential meaning of privacy as *the right to be and to become in childhood* allows for a more nuanced examination of childhood privacy and the necessary protection of the developing psyche. Exposure to privacy violations cause [*sic*] immense damage with far reaching consequences. While parents have a duty to protect their children, Black parents carry the additional burden of identifying and protecting their children from the predictable harms of racial discrimination.[29]

Indeed, when considering educational justice from a Black parent and home educator perspective, the primary focus will be on protecting children from the anti-Black context within, and outside, traditional schools as found in the existing literature. Therefore, Peters refers to Black home educators as "child privacy protectors," with *privacy* defined as the right to be and to become.[30] Likewise, this book defines educational justice from a Black home educator perspective as the pursuit and attainment of the right and freedom to be and to become. By choosing to home educate, Black parents necessarily pursue and attain their children's right and freedom to be and to become in the manner of their own choosing.

Therefore, Black home education today represents a resistance movement to gain educational justice for Black children in response to what past educational scholars and thinkers prophetically spoke of as the challenges that would, and for the most part have, come to fruition with the implementation of mandated desegregation of public schools. Horace Tate, who was the head of the Georgia Teachers and Educators Association in 1970 when the federal government forced the South into compliance with the 1954 *Brown v. Board of Education* mandate to desegregate public schools, gave a speech in which he prophetically declared what would indeed happen.[31] Tate referred to the desegregation plan as a "second-class integration illustrating the failure of school desegregation policies to meet the expectations of black educators and, further, to point out that their voices were being diminished."[32] Additionally, Carter G. Woodson, an educator and scholar ahead of his time, declared that had desegregation designers sincerely cared, they would have included a focus on African American cultural and historical connections in the curriculum from an asset-based perspective as well as the necessary teacher-student relationship, which had been crucial to Black student achievement for hundreds of years.[33] Many other Black educational and intellectual thinkers of the time attempted to forewarn us, but their voices did not move the decision makers of the time.

The Black scholars and thinkers of the past would not be surprised to find today's Black education riddled with challenges to educational attainment, disproportionality in the application of discipline, the school-to-prison pipeline, underachievement of Black youth, barriers to gifted education, frequent referral to special education, and even resegregated public schools. In addition to these learning hurdles, scholars have documented the anti-Black racism Black students experience through intentional or unintentional interactions with individual teachers, students, and administrators or through inequity in policy or policy enforcement.[34] If you are reading this, you are likely familiar with the longstanding dismal statistics associated with Black education and the deficit thinking that continues to be applied to Black children. The research literature has referred to schools as sites of Black suffering and described the "spirit murdering" of Black children within public schools.[35] Further, research has documented the disenfranchisement of Black parents, including middle-class Black parents, as they attempt to advocate for their children within school systems.[36] These are some of the reasons many Black families pursue educational justice for their children through home education.

PURPOSE AND OVERVIEW OF THE BOOK

Research on the ways in which home education has enabled Black parents to obtain educational justice for their children and how those strategies can inform traditional education remains sparse—hence the purpose and title of this book, *Creating Educational Justice*. As previously stated, the book is centered on the premise that if we want to know how to effectively educate Black children, we need to ask Black parents, whose perspectives have rarely been represented in school reforms, particularly those Black parents who have chosen to assume full responsibility for their children's education through homeschooling and have obtained their definition of educational justice as a result.

Creating Educational Justice departs from the existing research-based texts and memoirs on Black home education by intentionally interpreting Black families' experiences of and approaches to home-based learning to extrapolate key factors that inform best practices regarding Black students' learning needs, and the learning needs of all children. Unlike earlier texts, this book conceptualizes today's Black homeschooling as a form of educational justice; a method for overcoming the much researched and written-about ills associated with Black children's learning experiences in traditional schools. The major thesis of this text is that instead of working within school systems, Black parents who homeschool today create their own educational justice, and as teachers, administrators, and policy makers, we can learn from Black homeschool parents' decision-making and their educational practice.

Creating Educational Justice documents the experiences that led the interviewed Black families to homeschool, presents characteristics of the learning context parents created for their children, and then draws on the experiences of Black home educators to inform teacher education, school administration, and educational policy. Each chapter focuses on a major theme found in the data that is representative of educational justice. To embody educational justice, each chapter will feature a vignette created directly from the raw data gathered through the research. The vignettes are intended to provide readers with an example that illustrates the focus of each chapter in order to enhance understanding. Reading the statistics on discipline disproportionality is not nearly as powerful as listening to the voices of Black parents sharing their own experiences of attempting to advocate for a child who has been labeled a "troublemaker." Following the vignette, each chapter will discuss its theme as found within the data and in connection to pedagogy, news events, issues, or trends in popular, political, and professional discourse in education today, and it will offer an interpretation of how Black home educators' experiences provide responses and solutions to those issues.

WHAT'S COMING NEXT

Chapter 1, "The Diversity of Black Home Educators," provides a brief description of the research methods and context, while also presenting descriptions of the tremendous demographic diversity that exists among the sixty-three represented Black home education families. This chapter features tables to demonstrate the demographic diversity within Black homeschool families, including family structure, socioeconomic status, parents' educational level, number of children homeschooled, whether they left public or private schools or homeschooled from birth, and the grade level at which they entered homeschooling. This chapter provides an overview of the home educators represented throughout the book.

Chapter 2, "Black Home Education as a Pathway Toward Healing," outlines Black home educators' beliefs regarding how homeschooling has provided a pathway toward healing, which is an important outcome when homeschooling is conceptualized as a form of resistance and educational justice. Home educators describe ways in which homeschooling has fostered racial healing for their children and for their family. In addition, homeschooling has promoted other forms of healing, including intergenerational family healing and community healing. This focus on healing is critical to understand the impact of historical trauma on Black families and the lingering impact of anti-Black racism on Black families and communities.

Chapter 3, "Black Home Educator Folk Pedagogy as Putting Children First," describes Black home educators' pedagogical approach. Even though home educators chose a variety of approaches to homeschool, one thing each approach had in common was the placement of children at the center of their learning. This chapter relates these approaches to those of the educational theorists of the Progressive Era and today.

Chapter 4, "Former Black Teachers Choosing Home Education," discusses the phenomenon of Black teachers leaving their classrooms to become home educators, establish homeschool centers (homeschooling other people's children), or serve as homeschool consultants. The collective voices of Black teachers who have become home educators speak to today's teacher shortage and the challenges of retaining teachers of color. They also speak to the challenges and constraints teachers experience as professionals attempting to teach in ways they know all children need. These Black home educators seek educational justice through homeschooling, which provides them with the professional freedom they need to be the best teachers they can be.

Chapter 5, "Parents' Freedom to Choose How to Be Engaged," focuses on parents' descriptions of being marginalized or disenfranchised from engaging in their children's education within public or private schools. They describe the types of barriers they encountered as they attempted to advocate for their children. The chapter draws connections to research documenting the marginalization of Black parents and provides alternative effective strategies for collaboration with Black families, and all families.

Chapter 6, "Ubuntu and the Power of Community," examines the meaningful and powerful interdependent relationships Black home educators build within their communities. Whether they reside in rural, suburban, or urban communities, Black home educators incorporate community resources in their homeschool practice and, as a result, tend to strengthen their communities. The chapter explores how traditional schools might dovetail with these strategies.

The overarching focus of the book is Black home educators' insights on education, which are provided from a place of empathy regarding the pressures of schooling in traditional settings. The empathy Black home educators expressed for teachers and other public education professionals today will be explored in chapter 1.

CHAPTER 1

The Diversity of Black Home Educators

In 2004, Karyn and her husband, Charlie, had enrolled their firstborn, Terry, into a Christian-based preschool program while Karyn cared for their newly adopted twin babies. But as Terry approached his fifth birthday, Karyn began researching kindergarten options. She read about homeschooling, and the idea of educating all her children at home began to "burn in [her] heart." Karyn spent time at the library searching for additional information on home education. Then one day she approached her husband with the idea of homeschooling Terry, and he responded, "We are not the kind of people that do that." Consumed with passion for the idea of teaching him at home, Karyn quickly retorted, "Maybe we can become the kind of people who homeschool."

This exchange between Karyn and Charlie raises the question, What type of people homeschool their children? Ultimately, Karyn and Charlie did become a home education family. But one Black home education family cannot fully represent all Black home educators, nor can they represent all sixty-three Black families who participated in the research discussed in this book, among whom there was great diversity.

In my encounters, I have found that for some people, the word *homeschooling* continues to conjure images of radically antigovernment households, rigidly religious families, wealthy elite families, or different-in-some-way families like what Charlie imagined before he became a homeschool father. But my research shows that Black home education families represent a profusion of family demographics and characteristics beyond those limiting stereotypes.

Therefore, this chapter presents descriptive and demographic data to demonstrate the tremendous amount of diversity that existed among the Black home educating families represented in this research. The chapter dispels the notion of Black home educators being a monolithic group and the stereotypes associated with homeschool families generally. Moreover, it demonstrates the complexity of answering the question, Who in the Black community homeschools their children? Ultimately, this chapter demonstrates that Black home educators represent an eclectic group of people united by their embrace of the right to seek and create educational freedom for their children through homeschooling.

This chapter is organized to help readers understand the context of each research study and then become familiar with the sixty-three Black home educators through key features of the entire group. The chapter begins with a brief description of the varying contexts and aims of the three studies conducted between 2006 and 2021. Next, the sixty-three participating families are presented based on their point of entry (e.g., from birth, preK to second grade, third to fifth grades, and middle school and high school) into home education. This section provides data-based insight regarding the relationships between when a family decided to home educate and their motivations to do so. The next section presents demographic ranges and variations (e.g., income level, parents' education, family structure) among the sixty-three representative Black home education families based on the available data. Finally, the chapter closes with a description of the varied approaches to home education represented among the sixty-three Black homeschool families who participated in this research.

RESEARCH CONTEXTS

As a reminder, this research was conducted in three different studies between 2006 and 2021. Most of the families homeschooled long before the COVID-19 pandemic, but a few of the participants in later studies began their home education practice during the pandemic. Each of the three studies employed qualitative methods consisting of individual recorded interviews. Additionally, the initial study included three focus group sessions, while the other studies utilized Sister Circle methodology, which offered a more culturally relevant approach to the research process. Focus group sessions and Sister Circles provided validation, clarification, and expansion of thematic findings from the initial data analysis. Table 1.1 provides an overview of all three research studies conducted between 2006 and 2021.

TABLE 1.1 Overview of research studies conducted between 2006 and 2021

Dates	*Focus of the study*	*Number of families*	*States represented*	*Demographic differences*
2006–8	Why and how do Black parents homeschool their children or have they home-schooled their children in the past?	37 families total 7 single-parent households **Interviewees** 34 mothers 2 couples 1 divorced dad	Florida Georgia Maryland North Carolina Tennessee	**Income mean: $45,000–$55,000** Under $15,000–$25,000 = 4 $25,001–$45,000 = 8 $45,001–$65,000 = 14 $65,001+ = 11 **Parents' highest education** (72% college educated) High school = 4 Some college = 5 Undergraduate = 13 Master's = 11 PhD/JD/MD = 4
2018–19	How do Black home educators perceive their homeschool practice has served as a pathway toward healing?	12 mothers	Georgia Illinois Indiana Maryland New York North Carolina Pennsylvania Texas Wisconsin	(Income data not collected for this study) **Home educators' highest education** Some college = 1 Undergraduate = 2 Master's = 3 Doctorate = 5 JD = 1
2020–21	How do Black home educators in rural communities perceive the unique benefits, and challenges, of homeschooling in rural communities?	14 mothers	Alabama Arkansas California Georgia Louisiana Maryland North Carolina Pennsylvania Tennessee Texas	(Income data not collected for this study) **Home educators' highest education** Undergraduate = 3 Master's = 4 Doctorate = 6 JD = 1

Notes: Two home educators participated in more than one study. Due to missing data, this book reports on findings based on only sixty-three of the original seventy Black home educators.

As described in the introduction, the first study conceptualized home education as an extreme form of parental engagement in their children's education. This initial study was conducted over two years (2006–8) and concentrated on the Metro Atlanta area but expanded to include Florida, Maryland, and North Carolina. This expansion was undertaken because the recruitment strategy of community nomination (where participating home educators were asked to refer additional eligible families to participate in the study) revealed connections between Black home educators in Georgia and families in other states. This study broadly queried the motivations and practices of Black homeschool families. A total of thirty-seven Black families participated in this first study, including seven single-parent families. Participating families self-reported a mean annual income range of $45,000–$55,000. This range was below the median income level of $59,600 for the Metro Atlanta area at the time.[1] Thus, contrary to popular stereotypes, the Black home educators represented in this study were not primarily from elite or wealthy families, nor did they heavily represent upper-middle-income families in the area at the time the study was conducted. Instead, participating Black families represented working middle-income and lower-middle-class households. This classification is further corroborated by parents' self-reports of their highest level of education. Though 72 percent of the participating Black home educators were college graduates, only four out of the forty-six held advanced graduate or professional degrees (PhD, law degree, or medical degree), while nine parents reported having a high school diploma or some college. It should be noted that Georgia does not require parents to hold a college degree to homeschool their children. Most participating Black parents (twenty-four parents) held undergraduate or master's degrees. This is a significant finding given the longstanding racial disparity of Black incomes and the fact that choosing to homeschool frequently meant that Black families would also have to transition from a two-salary household to a one-salary household, usually sacrificing the mother's income and career.[2] Later in this chapter the varying points of entry of Black families will be discussed. A detailed description of these varying points of entry and parents' motivations to home educate will be provided later in this chapter.

The second study of Black home education began in 2018, ten years after the end of the first study. During this time, I conducted a comparative study with the late Monica Wells Kisura, who had conducted a dissertation study of Black home education in the Metro DC area.[3] Given the relatively large number of participants in the initial study, I did not have to recruit additional participants. All my publications during this time were based on the initial study. But by 2018, I began to wonder how the conceptualization of Black home education as a form of resistance specifically might also align with creation of a pathway toward healing, however Black home educators might define healing. Therefore, the second research study, conducted from 2018 to 2019, focused on understanding how Black home education might be conceived as a pathway toward healing from the perspective of Black parents. This study included twelve Black home educators representing nine different states. Two of these parents participated in the initial homeschool study from 2006 to 2008 as well. As can be seen in table 1.1, income data were not collected for this second study. Using community nomination, this second study's recruitment process yielded more families with mothers who held advanced or professional graduate degrees (five doctoral degrees and one law degree) than it did those with master's (three mothers) or undergraduate degrees (two mothers). Only one of the mothers had not completed a college degree. This is most likely due to the use of community nomination as a study recruitment technique, as the nomination process began with colleagues who were in higher education and had homeschooled their children. Though this study had a small number of participants, the findings were triangulated with data from the original study with regard to conceptions of healing. The results of this study will be fully presented in the next chapter.

Finally, table 1.1 presents a third research study conducted from 2020 to 2021, which queried the home education experiences of Black families living in rural communities because previous studies have focused on Black home education in large urban areas. The rural Black home education study was conducted with fourteen Black homeschool mothers representing ten states. Unlike Black home educators living in urban metropolitan areas, rural Black homeschool parents were not able to nominate additional Black home educators from their communities to participate in this research because they typically represented the only Black homeschool family in their communities. However, Black home educators were well connected via social media and other internet-based platforms, which is how ten states came to be represented in the study. Two of the fourteen mothers had participated in the study on Black homeschooling as healing as well. As shown in table 1.1, all the mothers held college degrees; seven had doctoral or professional degrees, four had master's degrees, and three had undergraduate degrees. Overall, the findings from this pilot study documented the benefits and challenges of being Black, homeschooling, and living in rural communities. These findings will be shared more fully in the demographic differences section of this chapter.

The sixty-three Black families represented within this book participated in at least one of the three research studies presented in table 1.1. From the foregoing brief description of each study, one can already observe the differences among the families and how this research dispels stereotypes of Black home education families and homeschool families overall. The next section introduces readers to the participating families, with an emphasis placed on the point within their children's educational journey that parents decided to homeschool.

CULTURAL DIVERSITY, HOME EDUCATION ENTRY POINTS, AND MOTIVATIONS

Cultural Diversity Among Black Home Educators

This research consistently employed a multiphase approach to interviewing.[4] As a result, each interview began with an exploration of the parents' upbringing, including where they grew up and how their parents or caregivers engaged in their learning. By unearthing their childhood experiences, many home educators drew connections between those experiences and how they decided to engage in their children's education, including their decisions to homeschool. Those influences can be positive or negative. Moreover, the inclusion of home educators' childhood experiences in this research revealed sharp contrasts in cultural beliefs. For example, 13 percent (eight Black home educators) shared that they were from Caribbean countries (e.g., Trinidad, Virgin Islands, Jamaica) and one Black home educator was a native of Great Britain. These Black ethnics came from countries whose residents hold beliefs about schooling that often differ from those found in the US. Some of these countries' beliefs highly favor home education. Further, research has suggested that Black ethnics or immigrants have more favorable experiences within the United States compared with those of native African American students, to the point that the former have been referred to as elevated minorities.[5] Though I have chosen not to focus on these essential differences here, it is interesting to note that mothers who are natives of Caribbean countries are found in the "homeschooling from birth" category or began home education in preK or kindergarten. Future research should focus entirely on the homeschooling experiences of Black immigrants in the US.

Defining Home School Entry Points

Parents decided to homeschool their children at different points in their children's education, and for varying combinations of reasons. Previous research on homeschooling has classified home educators as either ideologues or pedagogues.[6] Ideologues are parents who believe they should serve as their children's first educator, while pedagogues are parents who disagree with the teaching approaches found in traditional schools (public or private) and believe their children would benefit most from an approach to teaching that they themselves could provide. In the following, I use data from all three studies to present the sixty-three Black home educators by the points at which they entered homeschooling and the relationship between points of entry and Black parents' motivations to homeschool. Home educators' points of entry into homeschooling span four categories: from birth, preK–second grade (lower elementary school), third to fifth grades (upper elementary school), and middle school and high school. However, these categories are not necessarily linear.

As already shown in table 1.1, the parents represented in this text have differing demographics such as level of education and family income. Home educators' descriptions of when and why they began homeschooling their children also contained several complexities. In this section, I present these complexities as delimitations related to interpreting the data on home educators' motivations to educate their children at home and their points of entry into homeschooling. As delimitations, these characteristics are not necessarily included in the interpretation of findings but inform the definition of entry points in this research. Moreover, these characteristics have implications that future research should consider.

On the surface, determining the point at which a family began to homeschool their children would seem to be relatively uncomplicated. However, a definitive description of what "homeschooling from birth" means was needed because most of the parents who engaged in this research expressed some version of the sentiment, "I have always homeschooled my children." Therefore, for the purposes of this study, "homeschooling from birth" means parents began teaching their children at home from birth and those children had never attended formal or traditional schools of any type at the time of the study.

The point about children never having attended traditional schools of any kind became critical, because thirteen out of the sixty-three Black home educators intentionally moved their children in and out of homeschooling throughout their children's preK–12 educational experiences. For example, some parents talked about enrolling their children in preK and kindergarten programs specifically to help with their social-emotional development and then pulling them out for home education to build on that foundation. Private religiously based programs or focused programs such as Montessori ones were frequently chosen for this purpose. Some mothers also shared that they returned older children to public or private schools when they became pregnant with their subsequent children, when they adopted younger children into their families, or when the moms decided to go back to school. Still, other parents reported that they moved their children in and out of home education depending on the perceived quality of the schools they had access to when they moved to new cities or states. Financial challenges that required parents to return to work also led them to move their children in and out of home education. Finally, some parents gave their children the option to go to school and see how it went. Thus, in this text, the placement of a family in a point-of-entry category does not necessarily mean that the children remained in home education over the remainder of their educational journey.

Overlapping Motivations

Analysis of Black home educators' motivations to homeschool suggests that Black parents rarely decide to educate their children at home for one reason. Instead, they have multiple narratives and experiences that support their decisions. As the research has suggested, parents' decisions to homeschool are the result of factors that push them out of school and factors that pull them toward home education.[7] This complicates the attempt to identify single themes related to Black parents' home education decisions within each category of homeschool entry points. Instead, Black parents and their children have had unique experiences within different types of schools, varying beliefs regarding parents' roles in their children's education, different levels of self-efficacy in engagement in their children's education, and divergent concerns related to home educating, among other factors that influence decision-making. These factors combine in unique ways that will influence the degree of educational freedom experienced by Black parents who decide to homeschool. For this reason, in the next section key ideas related to Black home educators' motivations have been presented within each entry-point category with exemplars from the data.

DECIDING TO HOMESCHOOL FROM BIRTH

Black families who decided to begin homeschooling from birth made the decision before the baby was even born. Out of the sixty-three Black families, eleven families decided to homeschool their children from birth. Therefore, homeschooling represented the first-choice option for these families. These children also never attended public or private conventional schools at the time they participated in the research.

Table 1.2 provides an overview of Black home educators who chose to homeschool from birth, including their level of education, the number of children homeschooled, and how long they had been homeschooled at the time of the study

TABLE 1.2 Mothers who began home education from birth (*n* = 11)

*Home educator's name**	*Education*	*Number of children homeschooled*	*Years homeschooling*
Alana	Undergraduate	3	20+ years
Alayah	Master's	1 her own (+5 other children)	7 years
Jasmine	Master's	5	21 years
Kanesha	Undergraduate	4	10 years
LaTanya	Undergraduate	1	4 years
Moesha	Undergraduate	4	12 years
Monica	Postgraduate	5	14 years
Ranielle	Postgraduate	4	24 years
Shantal	Undergraduate	3	7 years
Simone	Undergraduate	3	7 years
Talisha	Undergraduate	5	18 years
		Total: 43 children homeschooled	Mean = 13 years

*Pseudonyms used for home educators' names.

they participated in. Out of the sixty-three families represented, eleven (18 percent) chose to homeschool their children from birth. One mother (Nichelle) had not completed college, while the others had undergraduate degrees (seven), master's degrees (three), or postgraduate degrees (two), meaning doctoral degrees or law or medical degrees. Combined, these eleven Black home educators taught a total of forty-three children. As indicated in table 1.2, Alayah, who is a former elementary school teacher, homeschooled her own child while also teaching five other children from different families in a homeschool school-like situation. The remaining families homeschooled their own children, ranging from one child up to five children. At the time of their interviews, the mothers had been homeschooling for an average of thirteen years, with a range of four to twenty-four years of home education experience. Alana, Jasmine, Ranielle, and Talisha had graduated at least one child from home education.

Based on existing literature, one might expect parents who decide to homeschool from birth to be motivated by foundational beliefs that contrast with the ideology of conventional schooling.[8] For example, parents who homeschool from birth would seem to share a belief that the home should be the primary site of education for children, not a government-run institution. Additionally, I wondered whether these parents might hold strong religious reasons related to their decision to homeschool compared with families who decided to homeschool later in their children's educational journeys.

Black parents who chose to homeschool their children from birth did so for three primary reasons (divine intervention or religious convictions, negative school reputation, and ideological conflict) intertwined with several contributing factors. As expected, these home educators held strong ideological beliefs regarding parents serving as the first and primary teachers. Surprisingly, though, only Alana and Monica conceptualized their homeschool motivation ideologies as the result of a direct instruction from their higher power. Alana shared, "For me, it was one of those. . . . I felt like God was telling me to do something. So I jumped at it once I was sure that's [homeschooling] what He [God] wanted me to do." Monica explained, "One thing is, I feel like it's a calling on my life to be home with the kids and to have as much involvement in their lives as I possibly can. I believe that we're stewards over God's children, and this time in my life I'm supposed to be focusing on them based on my view of God." While the other Black home educators did not specifically describe their decision to homeschool from birth as direct divine intervention, they did hold strong religious beliefs that supported their ideological conflict with conventional schooling. For example, Talisha explained her home education goals:

> We are raising them to be successful adults. . . . To have character is more important than books. I want them to have good character, make good decisions, be productive, responsible Americans, and those are some qualities that I've seen in some public schools, but they also teach things that we are not emphasizing. You know, tolerance, and all this other stuff. I want my kids to look at things through the filter of the Bible . . . and make decisions, you know—they say the way that Jesus would have—but you know, definitely using the character qualities that they talk about that are scriptural.

Such religious convictions served as a critical influence on home educators' "parents as the first teachers" ideology and therefore led to their decisions to homeschool from birth.

Black home educators also identified their motivations to homeschool as being based on reports—anecdotal and in the media—of negative experiences within schools and on ideology that conflicts with how schools operate as institutions.

Parents assumed a researcher role when it came to exploring educational opportunities for their children. Local and national media news reports of low-performing schools and school violence influenced eight of the eleven mothers' decisions to homeschool from birth. Friends also provided "insider" information on local schools. For example, Simone shared, "I had friends that had children that went to school, and they would come back with horror stories about the things that were going on in school like five-year-old kids trying to meet at the bus to kiss and all types of craziness and thirty-five kids per classroom and—it was just too much." LaTanya indicated that fear accompanied her decision to homeschool from birth: "But the other one is just the negative stigma that in recent years has been revealed about [her state's] education status at this point. And so it's coupled with the fear of my child becoming a statistic that's the norm here." The combination of personal accounts from friends who were public school parents and the negative media reporting greatly influenced Black parents' decisions to avoid public education.

Interestingly, parents' own schooling experiences also informed their ideologically based decisions to homeschool. Ranielle, a veteran home educator, recalled,

> We had read enough ourselves that we were not willing to take the risk, to put our children in government schools. And I'll use that word *government schools*—because government schools are government schools. . . . I think from our individual experiences, while we didn't think that our experiences were bad, we also didn't think that they were good enough for our children. One thing that was missing [in my school experience] was, it was never about me [*laughs*]. That may sound weird, but my educational experience was never about my interests. It was more about, you know, the school. . . . I just felt like every time I went to school, there was a new thing. Like, oh, we're rolling out the proficiency exam. We're rolling out the so and so. . . . It was like, I felt like a guinea pig all the time. And when I tell you I saw firsthand spirit murdering, I mean, normal happy-go-lucky people like me one day, and then the next day they have something in their hand [high school diploma] that doesn't afford them a chance to go to college.

Similarly, Simone and her husband reflected on their school experiences, and she shared, "When I look at schools, I didn't necessarily see them as preparing children for the world. I mean, like, we both attended college but by the time we got out of college, we couldn't start our own business." Overall, parents who homeschooled from birth did not believe in their locally assigned public school's ability to fully prepare their children to be successful in the world today. Interestingly, the public schools assigned to the families within this group had predominantly Black student populations (resegregated) and low resources compared with other schools in the district, which had more resources and predominantly White student bodies. Therefore, inequity in access to school choice options also influenced parents' decisions to homeschool from birth. Indeed, when asked about private school considerations, parents across income levels responded that their finances prevented private schools from being a viable option.

DECIDING TO HOMESCHOOL IN EARLY ELEMENTARY SCHOOL (GRADES PREK–2)

Black families who decided to homeschool when their children were in preK through second grade had enrolled their children in either private or public schools but removed them for a variety of reasons. Table 1.3 provides an overview of the twenty-three Black home education mothers represented in this category. Six participating mothers held undergraduate degrees, and seven held master's

TABLE 1.3 Mothers who began home education in preK–second grade ($n = 23$ families)

*Name**	*Entry point*	*Education*	*Number of children homeschooled*	*Years homeschooling*
Candy	PreK	Undergraduate	2	1 year
Connie	PreK	Master's	3	2 years
Jessica	PreK	Master's	2	7 years
Toni	PreK	Some college	2	6 years
Alyssa	K	Postgraduate	1	3 years
Amber	K	Undergraduate	6	10 years
Carla	K	Undergraduate	1	9 years
Hope	K	Master's	2	5 years
Kate	K	Postgraduate	2	1 year
Kendra	K	Postgraduate	1	12 years
Lucy	K	Undergraduate	2	13 years
Magnolia	K	Master's	2	5 years
Tambria	K	High school	4	14 years
Tempest	K	Master's	2	6 years
Annise	First grade	Undergraduate	1	1 year
Denise	First grade	Undergraduate	3	9 years
Janice	First grade	Postgraduate	3	16 years
Kimberly	First grade	Undergraduate	2	17 years
Shandra	First grade	Undergraduate	3	1 year
Sophie	First grade	Undergraduate	2	1 year
Camille	Second grade	Undergraduate	3	10 years
Megan	Second grade	Master's	2	5 years
Nancy	Second grade	Undergraduate	5	12 years
			56 total children homeschooled	Mean years homeschooling = 7 years

*Pseudonyms used for home educators' names.

degrees. Combined, these twenty-three Black home educators taught fifty-six children. Tambria and Nancy had the largest number of children with four and five children, respectively. Four families only homeschooled one child. Black families in this category had been homeschooling for a mean of eight years; ten of the mothers were in their first five years of homeschooling, while eight mothers had ten or more years of homeschooling experience. Within this category, most families began homeschooling in kindergarten (ten families), while four families decided to homeschool in preK, six families in first grade, and three families in second grade.

Hesitation to Homeschool

Interestingly, most of the mothers in this category (sixteen out of twenty-three home educators) demonstrated a preference for home education when they shared that they really wanted to homeschool their children from birth, but they hesitated. For example, Megan, who officially began homeschooling when her oldest child entered second grade, shared, "The ironic thing is that when my daughter was born, I had said that I was going to homeschool. That was a conversation that my husband and I had had, but then when it came time to do it, my faith just kind of waivered. And so instead I went to work full time on third shift to pay for my daughter to go to private school." Parents who hesitated to follow through with their plans to homeschool from birth frequently expressed feeling extreme pressure to "get it right" and not to "mess up" their kids. Shandra, who began homeschooling when her oldest entered the first grade, shared that she wanted to stay home to homeschool but felt she "wasn't qualified to teach her daughter at age three" and "wanted to make sure the foundation was laid properly" for her daughter, so she sent her to preschool and kindergarten before officially starting to home educate. For Megan, the hesitancy to homeschool represented a fear of "doing more damage than good." She shared, "I would rather pay someone who knows how to do it. . . . If I could afford it, I'd pay someone to homeschool them at home." Black home educators expressed feeling a lack of, or limited, self-confidence related to their homeschool practice, particularly in the first five years of homeschooling. The next section describes motivations that influenced mothers to overcome these hesitancies related to homeschooling.

Motivations to Begin Homeschooling in PreK–Second Grade

Black mothers' motivations to begin homeschooling in preK–second grade were the result of varying combinations of negative interactions in school, perceived racism in school, and a conflict between the sociopolitical context or pedagogical approaches of schooling and the specific needs of their children. Exemplars from the data follow to demonstrate the ways in which these layered motivations worked together to influence parents' decisions to homeschool in preK–second grade.

Negative Parent-Teacher Interactions, Sociopolitical Context, and Children's Needs. Mothers were moved toward home education when they perceived that their home-school relationship led to harmful situations for their children. In addition, the school environment, such as overcrowding or rigid school policies, blocked teachers' ability to fully meet their children's needs. For example, Shandra, who initially felt unqualified to teach her daughter at age three, sent her child to a public preK and kindergarten. She felt that the pressure to "get it right" was too much and preferred to focus on being a mother. Problems began when she found that her daughter was ahead of the curriculum taught in kindergarten. The school tried to accommodate her daughter's advanced academic level by putting her in a higher grade for half of the day, hoping to keep her challenged, but she threw temper tantrums because she did not want to leave the kindergarten class. While she was academically advanced, her emotional maturity was not. Shandra shared that her daughter "began to miss out on some things at school due to her behavior, which the school referred to as emotional immaturity." Her daughter became identified as having a behavior problem. Shandra soon came to believe that "keeping her in that class was a waste of her mind and it was making [her] lazier. Keeping [her] in school would be like drinking water even when you know it is contaminated." Shandra's likening the school to contaminated drinking water indicates that she viewed homeschooling as a way to rescue her daughter from harm. The classroom teachers' emphasis on Shandra's daughter's behavior instead of her academic abilities led Shandra to negatively view her school-parent interaction.

Other examples of negative school-parent interactions that influenced parents' decisions to educate at home in preK–second grade emerged in the data. When Amber's oldest child was in kindergarten, Amber attended a parent-teacher conference where she was told that her daughter was not reading and therefore would have to be retained in kindergarten. Amber shared,

> I said, "In kindergarten?" "She's not reading well enough to be promoted," [the teacher] said. And I said, "But when was she supposed to start reading? Who's supposed to teach her?" You know? At least I taught her ABCs, I taught her numbers and stuff like that, so what's the teacher going to do? And so I said, "Well

> are there any students in your class reading?" . . . And I'm thinking, well, I thought I was doing well to just get her ready and then the teacher would do the rest. That's what I was thinking. So they wanted to hold her back, but I told them, "No. Since I know what you expect, then I'll work with her over the summer, but I want her to keep on going." Then I just kept her out because I realized that they weren't really teaching my child. That's what the problem was.

Here, the negative encounter between parent and teacher appears to have been based on misconceptions of expectations for kindergarten and misunderstandings about the parent and teacher roles. Amber also expressed a concern that teachers do not have enough time to spend with each child, as the kindergarten class is rather large at close to thirty students. Carla made similar remarks regarding her daughter's kindergarten experience. She stated, "She [her daughter Chelsea] wasn't understanding because the teacher has, you know, thirty kids and you can't teach to everybody's learning style and apparently that teacher's teaching style didn't match with Chelsea's learning style. So she would bring home her work and I got to re-teach it." In both situations, Black home educators expressed a sense of empathy for the teachers' situation with large class sizes but simultaneously expressed dissatisfaction in their children's academic progress because of those large class sizes.

Black home educators' understandings of the sociopolitical context surrounding their children's locally assigned schools also influenced their decisions to homeschool. Camille reported,

> I realized that the school system here was very segregated. And so, where race was a concern, that was one of the decisions we had to make based on that.
>
> Where we live . . . , the school systems are very overcrowded. You find a lot of people in my neighborhood . . . [whose] kids are bused to the north side of town. It's supposed to be the same education on both sides of the district, but it's not the same. They are bused to the north because parents want a better type of education for their children. I mean, the education is different on the north side of town. It's better. But it comes at a sacrifice for the family on the south side because they must get up extra early—I mean, these kids have to get up and be at the bus stop by six o'clock in the morning!

Unlike the other families in the neighborhood whose children had gained access to the better-resourced schools in the northern part of the school district, Camille's family was not willing to make the sacrifice of less family time. The commute to and from school would have extended the school day by an hour or more, which would have drastically cut into time with her children. Camille's family prioritize family time, and therefore busing their children to better schools in the northern part of the district was not an option for them.

Conversely, Dahlia, a mother who enrolled her son in four different public schools before turning to home education, gave up access to a "good" school in the northern portion of the school district with high hopes of supporting a new charter school that was opening in the southern, underresourced, resegregated segment of the school district where she lived. Her account is detailed elsewhere.[9] But when the new charter school failed, Dahlia turned to homeschooling as "a last resort." Trying to navigate the sociopolitical boundaries proved to be time consuming and impossible for Dahlia. Like other moms who entered home education between preK and second grade, Dahlia found that transitioning to home education gave her the necessary ability to overcome inequity issues within the system and negative parent-teacher relationships.

Impact of Anti-Blackness Within Schools on Children's Racial Self-Identity.

Black mothers perceived racism or anti-Blackness, whether intentional or unintentional, within their children's traditional school environments, both public and private. At times, parents observed adverse changes in their children's self-identity, which they attributed to their children's school environments. Annise's case provides an example of this. Annise is the mother of three children. Her two oldest children were adults, and they had been educated in her native home, the Virgin Islands. But when we met, Annise was a widow living in a rural community in the north. After enrolling her six-year-old son in a private preschool and then a public kindergarten program, Annise started homeschooling him because of changes she had observed in him. With much emotion, Annise shared, "I noticed he's wondering why is he different? He came home one day and said if he keeps his hands in water . . . it will turn white. So he started wondering like, what's wrong with me? So, he, he has this . . . he feels something's wrong with him." The community Annise lived in was only 4 percent Black, and the school her son attended did not have any Black teachers; they had Black cafeteria workers and bus drivers. She identified this lack of diversity as part of the issue. Annise further explained, "I saw certain behavioral issues with him and him trying to figure out why certain people won't play with him and different things like that. So that's not what I want for him. I want what my daughters had. But being that I am in the States, I don't really have that community around me. . . . I need to have diversity around me. So I'm planning on moving. But that's my motivation to homeschool. He needs a different environment." Annise assumed that the lack of diversity in the school led to her son's racial self-hate, and seeing this led Annise to feel the need to remove him from that destructive educational setting.

Research has also demonstrated that seemingly benign instructional strategies, such as the traffic light with clips used in many classrooms to monitor student behavior, can become racialized in adverse ways for children of color not only in terms of their behavior but also by sending negative messages regarding their intelligence.[10] Teachers may not even be aware of the negative impact such ubiquitous behavior management strategies have on students of color. But Black parents' observations of changes in their children's racial self-identity and their internalized racism contributed to decisions to homeschool. Black home education provided parents with a way to stop the damage, begin to undo the harm, and prioritize a process of reestablishing a positive Black identity for children as a pursuit of educational justice for them.

Pedagogical Conflicts. Another insight found in parents' motivations to homeschool beginning in preK through second grade concerned rigid expectations found in some private early childhood classrooms. Black home educators expressed discontent when they discovered that the preschool or kindergarten they had enrolled their children in demonstrated what they considered "unrealistic" or "developmentally inappropriate" classroom requirements. Toni, for example, described being disturbed by what she saw in the private Christian kindergarten program in which she had placed her daughter:

> The curriculum requires them to sit at the desk, raise their hands at lunch. . . . You know, be quiet and stand in the hall, in the line, don't move, hands to your side. And the teacher kept telling me, she [her daughter] seemed immature; she wanted to keep her back. And I told her, I said, "Well, she's born in the latter part of the year." At that point she had had her the whole year. And so . . . I was amazed. To me, I thought she should have been familiar with all her students or first she should have gone and assessed, you know, the possibility as to why she [her daughter] was, you know, immature compared to some of the other kids. And she told me, she said, "Oh, she is born—she's born in the latter part of the year?" . . . So we let her finish that year out and then we took her out.

Homeschooling provided a way to avoid having her daughter be required to repeat kindergarten because she was deemed "too immature," when it was more than likely that the classroom setting lacked the flexibility needed to teach young children. All five-year-old children simply are not the same. Attendance policies usually have cutoff ages for when children can begin these early grades, but those birthdates do not necessarily guarantee a certain level of maturity in a child. Some might even ask, What is a fair or accurate expectation of a preK- or kindergarten-age student? Additionally, how can educational professionals recommend retention of a child based on a lack of maturity if the child has demonstrated grade-level understanding of subject area content? Should kindergarten teachers be expected to know when their students were born, given school policies surrounding birthday cutoff dates for admission?

The challenges in pedagogical conflicts identified by Black home educators suggest issues related to rigidity in school policies. When parents choose home education, they gain the freedom to employ instructional approaches that meet their children's maturity and academic needs. Homeschool parents can give their children breaks as frequently as needed. Sometimes children need more than one recess in the day, and they often benefit from brain breaks between subjects. In contrast, public schools tend to have fixed recess schedules to accommodate the many demands on often limited play space. Homeschooling also enables parents to effectively support children whose academic performance in one subject is advanced though they may struggle in other subjects. As seen in some of the other situations discussed earlier in this chapter, schools sometimes lack the ability to support children who perform above grade level in one subject but not the others. The rigidity in policy and procedures that parents experienced in public school may have been a symptom of the emphasis on test scores necessitated by the 2001 No Child Left Behind legislation.

Other types of pedagogical conflicts emerged in the experiences of Black home educators related to public schools' emphasis on test scores. We have already seen one such experience shared in the introduction's vignette, for example. The Robinsons disliked the idea of their daughter's first day of kindergarten being consumed with paper-and-pencil tests, and so did their daughter. Overall, the Black parents represented in this study, whether interviewed in the 2006–8 study or the more recent ones, prioritized instilling a love of genuine learning in their children over testing performance. Carla captured the prominent perspective of Black home educators on testing, standards, and instilling a love of learning in children:

> A lot of teachers, now they have this testing requirement "teach for the test." And the kids don't remember what it [the subject] was, because one, it wasn't memorable. Two, it was just for the test so I'm cramming it in for that and then I can forget it 'cause I'm not gonna be tested on it again. Three, I have no lifelong understanding of how that applies to my life and what it is that I'm gonna use it for. That again goes back to making learning fun. When we did ancient Egypt, we didn't just read history books about Egypt, we didn't read her age level. We went to the kids' section and got the fun books because they have the same information; they just do it differently and they present it with more fun. Then we went to her teen level and got reading books, fiction books, that were set in those time periods and she read those. We were doing Rome and that's where we will start back. She had read the Roman history, so when we were doing Rome, she was like, "Oh yeah, this guy was there in such-and-such and he said that da-da-da-da."'Cause she can connect it, and to me that's more important because that shows her understanding versus memorization.

Like Carla, other Black parents sought to ensure their children would enjoy the learning process, and they approached instruction in ways that not only did this but also encouraged their children's discovery or connection building as they learned. Memorization and regurgitation of facts was kept to a minimum, if used at all.

Black parents often consulted state standards for each subject area in the grade levels they taught, but in this research, they always found state standards represented content that their children had already learned. In other words, by being able to meet their children's academic needs, Black home educators can teach their children beyond state content area standards. Magnolia, who based her instruction primarily on Montessori's child-centered approach, exemplifies this perspective of the state standards. She explained,

> Well, to me, Georgia is basing it on, like, "Okay, this is kindergarten; this is what you need to know." What Montessori is saying is, "Okay, this is the child's age, and so therefore this is what MOST children developmentally are able to do by this age." So the Montessori philosophy is that the child has from kindergarten to third grade to learn this material. So there's no stressing the child to, like, "Okay, you know this child is in kindergarten, so they should know how to count," because they would say they will be exposed to this again in first grade. So I kind

> of look at both of those and based on what I feel our child can do, that's how I adjust our goals. But usually, it's still always ahead of the state of Georgia curriculum.

The Montessori approach to teaching and learning places children at the center of their education. It is a philosophy, developed during the Progressive Era in the early 1900s, that is based in John Dewey's theory of constructivism, which explains that people learn by building connections between new ideas and previous understandings, as well as through lived experiences.[11] By modeling their home education practice after the Montessori philosophy of learning, Magnolia and her husband were able to teach to their children's abilities rather than standards or tests.

In comparison, teachers often feel compelled to teach to the state standards, not beyond them.[12] As a teacher educator, I have taught courses with preservice teachers who also had a weekly field placement in schools connected to our face-to-face class. During our time together, students reflected on the contradictions they observed between the theories they were learning in our class and what happened in their assigned classrooms. As an example, two students who were paired together in the same classroom shared that their mentor teacher started a new unit on Native American tribes. They observed students' excitement about the topic. But when a student asked if they could learn about the Seminoles because that was the name of the football team he played on, the teacher responded, "No, that's not one of the six tribes on our list." My budding teachers realized this was a missed opportunity to engage this student and any other students who had heard of the Seminoles or other tribes not represented in the state standards.

Interestingly, the theories of teaching and learning taught in my teacher education courses for the most part align with ideas supporting constructivism. My emerging teachers knew that instead of ignoring the student who asked about the Seminoles, a more effective approach would have been to ask the student what he already knew about the Seminoles and what he wanted to learn about them. Then they would ask their students what other Native American tribes they had heard of and what they knew about them as well. The unit would begin from their students' point of interest in Native American tribes and then incorporate the six tribes represented in the state standards for comparison purposes. Yes, this would take a little longer. But students' natural curiosity would drive the instruction, they would in turn be more engaged in their learning, and learning would be accomplished through a memorable stance of discovery rather than memorization of facts. Teaching would extend beyond the state standards in this approach, and students would learn to direct their own learning.

Black parents who chose to homeschool in preK through second grade sought pedagogical approaches that would maintain their children's interests and needs in learning. For Black parents, then, educational justice represents having the freedom to teach in ways that go beyond state standards and beyond content found on state tests. Educational justice requires flexibility, as well as truly knowing students' needs and caring enough to address those needs. Further, educational justice requires us to pay attention to how children experience teaching and learning, taking care to foster students' contributions to their learning and encouraging them to own their own learning.

DECIDING TO HOMESCHOOL IN THIRD TO FIFTH GRADES

As with the previous two entry points, a diverse set of parents decided to enter home education during the upper elementary years, third through fifth grades. Table 1.4 provides an overview of the fifteen Black home educators represented in this category. Eight of the mothers held undergraduate degrees, while four of them had master's or postgraduate degrees. Three of the mothers had some college but had not completed their degrees. Homeschool families who entered home education in the upper elementary grades ranged in number of children from one to ten. Most families had two or three children (eight out of fifteen families), and five families had four or more children. Two families had one child. Black homeschool mothers who chose to homeschool in the upper elementary grades had been homeschooling for an average of eight years at the time of the study. Five of the fifteen mothers had been homeschooling for ten or more years. Seven of the fifteen mothers were in their first five years of home educating. Shanelle, Bonita, and Dahlia were single mothers at the time of the research. Shanelle, Janice, Charlise, and Beverly worked full time outside their home as they homeschooled their children.

Given that the families in this category remained in public or private traditional schools longer than parents in the previous categories, I expected to find motivations based on a pattern of negative teacher-parent interactions or parents' perception of destructive policies and practices within traditional schools. In other words, I theorized that Black parents who had remained in traditional schools into the upper elementary grades may have experienced patterns of emotionally drain-

TABLE 1.4 Mothers who entered home education in third to fifth grades (*n* = 15 mothers)

*Name**	*Entry point*	*Education*	*Number of children homeschooled*	*Years homeschooling*
Bonita	Third grade	Some college	10	15 years
Cache	Third grade	Undergraduate	5	5 years
Charlise	Third grade	Master's	5	20+ years
Dahlia	Third grade	Master's	1	7 years
Jenae	Third grade	Some college	3	4 years
Robin	Third grade	Some college	1	3 years
Shanelle	Third grade	Postgraduate	2	1 year
Venisha	Third grade	Undergraduate	2	15 years
Beverly	Fourth grade	Undergraduate	7	20+ years
Callie	Fourth grade	Undergraduate	2	7 years
Nakia	Fourth grade	Undergraduate	3	12 years
Glenna	Fifth grade	Undergraduate	4	4 years
Janice	Fifth grade	Postgraduate	2	1 year
Venera	Fifth grade	Undergraduate	2	9 years
Victoria	Fifth grade	Undergraduate	2	1 year
			52 total children homeschooled	Mean years homeschooling = 8

*Pseudonyms used for home educators' names.

ing interactions as they attempted to advocate for their children within traditional schools. These parents also likely had deep, meaningful connections to other families who were homeschooling, which gave them intimate knowledge of the possibilities of home education. I found that home education represented parents' second choice, and it was even sometimes more of a third choice because parents would have chosen private education had they been able to afford it.

Homeschooling Not on Their Minds

Interestingly, like other home educators represented in the previous entry points, Black parents in this category knew other homeschool families but still did not decide to homeschool until later in their children's education. Parents who began home education in the upper elementary grades shared that initially homeschooling did not seem possible or even desirable for their family for a variety of reasons. The predominant reason Black home educators did not immediately consider home education was that they initially thought they should, or had to, make for their children the same choice that had been made for them, which was to attend public schools. There was an overall sense of trust that "it worked for me so it should work for my children." Additionally, Victoria shared, "I didn't know it [homeschooling] was an option, to be honest with you." When asked what made her turn toward home education, she explained, "I just took it upon myself to say if I'm already teaching my kids because they come home with every subject and I'm doing every subject all over again what is the point for them to go to school? There was no point. They were coming back home with everything. You ask them what they learned in school, and they say well it is in the book. So we have to read it all over again. So that didn't make any sense to me." Her observation of her children's inability, or unwillingness, to share what they had learned in school spurred her into reteaching, which ultimately led her to realize she was already educating her children at home.

Glenna, who was homeschooling her four children, described the different path that led to her decision to home educate: "I had been influenced over a pretty long period of time. But I had just not made that decision because in my mind homeschooling was not for me. I had no interest whatsoever in homeschooling [*slight chuckle*] because I was pretty much career minded." Her mother had even tried to get her to go into education, but Glenna declared, "I had no interest in that. But I guess just to honor her I did take one course in education when I first entered college. And I thought, 'This is not for me!' I just . . . I do not see myself with children all day. I could not see that picture." Instead, Glenna established her career in accounting. Yet she found herself surrounded by homeschooling families and observed the way homeschooled children carried themselves. Glenna explained, "I was impressed by the children, certainly nothing that their parents had verbally said to me, but I was impressed with the children. With the 'product,' you know, with the fruit that they were producing." These observations sparked her interest in home education.

Like Glenna, Bonita said, "You know this may seem strange, but I didn't want to homeschool. I was very much involved in my children's schools. My two daughters were in a small private school and so I was very much involved because I really wanted the togetherness." Her engagement at the school enabled her to closely monitor curriculum and instruction as well. However, conflicts between her family's moral standards and the school curriculum prompted her to consider homeschooling. As an example, Bonita explained,

> When my oldest son was in fourth grade, they were going to tell them, in a very mild way is what they told me, about sexuality. I'm looking at him [her son] and he was so very playful that he could care less about any of that information. It just didn't seem like a good time for him. When I talked to them at the school, they tried to explain to me that it wasn't going to be a big deal. But I said, "No, I don't like that idea. I think that should be left up to his father and I. We should be able to gauge when he is ready for that." After they had already agreed to do it with all the other children, my son said all the little boys were saying such bad things after viewing the film and listening to the talk. And that just didn't make sense to me. For them to be giving information to children when . . . who determined that that was the appropriate time? We're talking about young people growing up and I'm thinking that maybe the parents should determine that.

Bonita observed the impact of the instruction in her children at home. She said, "Whenever they came home, I was always sort of 'washing them up from the day.'" Here, Bonita was referring to her parental engagement role as requiring her to reorient her children's moral foundation. She clarified, "As far as my faith was concerned, that [having to "clean" the children daily] was important. Just on the moral standards that we have. I really wanted to instill those in the kids. The cleaning up then from the school day was me putting back in the moral standards damaged by the way things are presented in school and how the children responded." It was this experience that prompted her to look more closely into home education.

While their specific reasons for turning to home education are diverse, ranging from a perceived lack of learning to moral conflicts, overall, one of the reasons parents waited until the upper elementary school grades to homeschool their children was a belief or assumption that attending their local public school or going to a private school were their children's only options, or what they were "supposed" to do. The formation of this belief could be partially explained by parental role construction theory, which states parents make decisions on how to parent based on what they experienced as children.[13] But beyond this, Black parents' observations of perceived insufficiency in their children's education or their observations of relative success among home-educated students spurred their emotions and led them to choose home education.

Prominence of Race and Racism as a Motivating Factor

Black parents who entered home education in the upper elementary grades identified concerns with race or racism as a major factor in their decision to educate their children at home. These racialized motivations stemmed from an overarching perspective of Black education in the US or their specific experiences within schools.

Research on Black home education has reinforced the theory that teachers' instructional approaches matter a great deal to how children see the world and themselves. We should never underestimate the power and influence of our instruction, whether effective or ineffective. Janice shared,

> The more I've spoken to colleagues that are Black women raising Black children, the more we realize that schooling for our children is simply put on the back burner in most schools. Instead, they really want . . . they try to make our children assimilate to the White culture, this cultural Whiteness. And I just rather, or I prefer to, teach my own children because for one I can include history that I know is accurate. I can be sure that they're learning things that I know they need, not just necessarily things that will be on a test, right? But things that I know will be of importance to them and that they will need to know about. I think it's important for [my sons] they learn content like math, but also things they don't get at school like things that are a part of our culture or things that are a part of our community that we're currently in, they don't get it. For example, [her son's] teacher read a book or maybe showed him a video. I can't remember, but he came home, and we were talking about the continents, and he said, "Well, I definitely wouldn't want to live in Africa." So I said, "Why, why would you not want to live in Africa?" And he said, "Well, [the teacher] read us a book"—or maybe they showed a video, I cannot remember—"and they [Africans] are very poor over there. And the children don't have lots of food." And so it's those types of things, because then you create self-hate, right? Because I'm like, uh, no, Cameron, that's just simply not true. That is a snippet of Africa. And not only that, because then he went into that's why he felt like—you know, this is *my* ten-year-old talking—and he felt like, slavery did the Black people good because they saved us from Africa, serious business! I laid that teacher out! But that's—that is the danger. That is the danger of White teachers for one who have no idea how to teach Black and Brown students and particularly Black kids. So, you know, I made sure to, you

> know, let Cameron know. I've tried to clean it up as much as possible at this point . . . the damage. But, you know, it's hard to change that perspective of them for them because they've seen it in a video, or they've heard it in a book. And I'm like, "Cameron, do you know that people in America suffer from malnutrition and food shortages, too?" And he was just like, "Well, um, whatever, [Teacher] had showed them or told them about Africa."

Janice described her work as a Black home educator as having to "clean up the damage" caused by the ineffective instruction of her son's teacher. She further defined her home education practice as "advocacy, really, and just making sure that my boys don't get stuck in this [school-to-prison] pipeline or don't get stuck in tracking." But her son appeared somewhat resistant to accepting his mom's perspective and seemed to prioritize what he learned in school. This is part of why Black parents engage in an unschooling or deschooling process.[14] Once schools have socialized our children into a White perspective of the world, self-hate or internalized racism can become established in them and follow them to adulthood.[15]

Self-hate and internalized racism were well documented during the infamous *Brown v. Board of Education of Topeka* case that resulted in the school desegregation mandate.[16] Using Black and White dolls, Kenneth Clark had children select which doll was the "good" doll and which doll was the "bad" doll. Repeatedly, Black children selected the White doll as good and the Black doll as bad. Sadly, the narratives of Black home educators demonstrate that nothing much has changed. Internalized racism and self-hate can just as easily be infused into Black children's schooling experiences today.

DECIDING TO HOMESCHOOL IN MIDDLE SCHOOL AND HIGH SCHOOL

The Black home educators represented in this study who decided to homeschool in the sixth to tenth grades expanded stereotypical notions of homeschool families. Usually, we think of a family beginning to homeschool when their children are young, but twelve families in this research began their home education practice during their children's sixth through tenth grades, when content becomes more complex. These preteen and teenage years would seem to be the worst time to try to assume the role of your child's teacher because of adolescents' opposition and resistance to seemingly any form of control. Yet families shared compelling motivations for their decisions to homeschool even at this age range.

TABLE 1.5 Mothers and a father who entered into homeschooling in middle grades and high school ($n = 12$)

Name	*Entry point*	*Education*	*Number of children homeschooled*	*Years homeschooling*
Mickey	Sixth grade	Undergraduate	1 of 2	3 years
Monisha	Sixth grade	Postgraduate	2	2 years
Patricia	Sixth grade	Postgraduate	2	2 years
Portia	Sixth grade	Undergraduate	1 of 2	2 years
Susan	Sixth grade	Postgraduate	1 of 4	2 years
Tamara	Sixth grade	Master's	1	2 years
Wendy	Sixth grade	Undergraduate	1	1 year
Violet	Seventh grade	Master's	6	5 years
Yolanda	Seventh grade	Some college	1 of 2	2 years
Carol	Eighth grade	Undergraduate	1 of 2	5 years
Ben	Ninth grade	Postgraduate	1 of 2	1 year
Sandra	Tenth grade	Master's	2	3 years
			Total children homeschooled = 20 children	Mean years homeschooling = 2.5 years

*Pseudonyms used for participants' names.

Moreover, families that began home education in middle school and high school also did not follow the usual pattern of homeschooling all their children. As shown in table 1.5, half of the twelve families homeschooled only one of their children. While one child was homeschooled, the other attended a traditional school (public or private). Interestingly, in each of the six cases (Mickey, Portia, Susan, Yolanda, Carol, and Ben) of split-schooling, the homeschooled child was a male. Yolanda explained, "I've seen the difference in that my oldest is a conformer and my youngest is a nonconformer. Nonconformers don't work in public schools. Because they don't fit in the little boxes that they have." In split-schooling families, the children who remained in traditional schools had acclimated to the school culture and they were having relative success. Conversely, the homeschooled siblings had challenges related to peer pressure, behavior, or academics.

Table 1.5 provides an additional overview of the twelve home educators in this category. Most of the families (seven out of twelve) began homeschooling at the start of the middle grades (sixth grade). Two parents began homeschooling when their oldest child began seventh grade, while one parent entered home education when their oldest child started eighth grade. The remaining two home educators began their practice while their children were in high school (ninth and tenth grades). One-third of the twelve home educators in this category (four home educators) held postgraduate degrees, while another one-third of the group had undergraduate degrees. The remaining third consisted of three parents with master's degrees and one mother with some college. The parent who had some college was working toward completing her undergraduate degree at the time of the study. Parents who began homeschooling during the middle grades and high school had been home educating for an average of 2.5 years, fewer years compared with parents in the other entry points.

Peer Pressure, Bullying, and Children's Requests

Black parents started homeschooling in grades 6–10 for a variety of reasons. Surprisingly, for Carol, Mickey, and Susan, their children asked to be homeschooled. Carol, who homeschooled one of her two children, shared,

> He [her son] asked to be homeschooled, and it had been something I had considered because my first encounter with home schooling was actually when my kids were before kindergarten. I met two African American homeschoolers. The thought intrigued me, and I had read quite a bit about it, and after elementary school, he had really asked to be homeschooled, but we didn't do that for the seventh grade. But at that point, I thought I would go back to work because I had been a stay-at-home mother. So I did go back to work while he was in the seventh grade, but that was a tough transition year for him in middle school, and he hadn't quite found a niche, and I thought because of the amount of time I was spending up at his middle school that perhaps it was time to give homeschooling a try . . . because he had asked and it sounded like he would be a happier person.

As Carol indicated, even when she went back to work full time, she had to find time to volunteer at the middle school in order to remain in touch with her children's education and well-being. Carol described her son's desire to be homeschooled in the context of the transition from a K–6 elementary school into a middle school. She stated,

> I think, and unfortunately I think this might be the case—in the sixth grade he had a small group of friends. We lived in a predominantly African American county and the school system is even more so predominantly African American, so there wasn't any racial tension. But then suddenly there became a lot of tension between the kids who were trying to do the right thing at school and those who weren't so much interested in doing the right kinds of things in school. At the end of the sixth grade, this group of friends he had, none of them were going to be going—they were all going to different middle schools, and he had [trouble], I think at that point, because he didn't really want to go to face an unknown.

Carol's family had remained close to the two homeschool families they had met, and this is how her son knew about home education as a possibility. By homeschooling he could avoid the awkwardness of entering middle school and avoid peer pressure to do things that he knew would not be acceptable in school. Carol's older daughter did not want to be homeschooled, so Carol and her husband honored their daughter's decision to remain in her high school and they split-schooled.

Ben, a divorced father who supported his then wife in deciding to homeschool one of their sons, reported doing so as a way of sheltering their son from the peer pressure and discipline issues. He explained, "It [reasons they decided to homeschool] was a couple of things, I think the first one was he wasn't doing well in the classroom setting. We had some disciplinary problems. We knew he was a very intelligent person, so we knew it wasn't because he couldn't do the work. And he wasn't getting good grades, so we thought that an alternative approach would be appropriate." Before deciding to homeschool, Ben and his wife at the time tried to partner with school staff to best support their son. He described, "We worked with the teachers trying to find out where there was a gap, you know . . . with things such as completing homework or taking tests and doing good on them, so we met with the teachers on several occasions, met with the principal, you know, the whole staff basically, trying to work with them. We did progress reports to keep on track as much as we could to at least get him on track to make sure he doesn't fail." Ben expressed empathy for the public school staff in response to a question about the effectiveness of working with school staff. He shared, "I would say to the best of their ability they were responsive. I say that hesitantly because I don't think they are equipped to deal with such a wide variety of learning styles because they were trained—or socialized—to teach in a certain way so on one level they have the content knowledge but maybe not necessarily the technique or the wisdom on how to implement the techniques for different learning styles, if you know what I'm saying." Here, like Yolanda, Ben indicates an understanding of public schools' limitations in meeting the learning needs of every type of student. Yet Ben shared that the homeschooling lasted for only a year because his son "wanted to get back in the school. I guess he thought it was going to be easy. I'll get to stay home, but I guess he found out that it was rougher. [*Laughter*] Yeah. Mom cares more than school. So he wanted to get back in school. I think he missed his friends. He's a very sociable person. Missed his friends. He wanted to do sports too and I had no knowledge of how to go about doing that when we were homeschooling him, so we let him go back." Unlike Carol's son, Ben's son did not buy into, or desire, home education. In this age group, students' motivations to be homeschooled would also seem quite critical.

For Susan, a home educator who homeschooled one of her four children, home education became necessary after several failed attempts to partner with school staff to resolve an issue with bullying. Because of the school's zero-tolerance policies, her son would be suspended for fighting even though he was the victim of bullying behavior. In describing her motivations to homeschool, Susan referenced the 2020 incident in which a White woman, Amy Cooper, called 911 on a Black man, Christian Cooper, who was birdwatching in Central Park, when he asked her to put her dog on a leash. Susan explained,

> I was processing, again, why we homeschool our current teenager. Then also thinking about, do we need to do this for our other children? Because I was thinking about the assault on Black children in the classroom. I just feel all kinds of emotions about that because my children have experienced the Amy Coopers in the classroom, be it in an educator or a student. So this one child that we do homeschool has felt that; he has experienced that, and we had to have some conversations with him about this. We send him to school and then he comes home, and we're having to unlearn those things that were shared with him or things that were done to him in the classroom. I also think we're in a school district where Amy Coopers show up, Amy Cooper–like behavior. We see that in the statistics in terms of behavior and discipline as well as academic performance. So, for my son, he was in the discipline number, and it was at that point that we realized this is

> not going to be his narrative. He's not going to be a part of the statistics. For that, we need to remove him from this space. He needs to be in a space where learning is the focus and not necessarily the discipline piece, but it was high numbers of low performance among African American boys. So that was our reasoning for wanting to do this [homeschooling].

Susan and her husband tried to work within the school, but that was not effective in resolving the bullying issue her son experienced. This, coupled with Susan and her husband's concern regarding the school district's dismal performance with Black male students, led to their decision to split-school.

Overall, the motivations of Black home educators who entered homeschooling during the middle grades and high school indicate breakdowns in home-school partnerships. How long should parents continue to work with schools to resolve harmful issues such as bullying, peer pressure, or anti-Blackness? In grades 6–10, home education provided Black parents with the opportunity to remove impediments to their children's learning and well-being.

This chapter has provided an overview of the diverse demographics and motivations among the Black home educators represented within this research. The chapter has also presented key features in Black parents' motivations to homeschool within four categories based on their points of entry into home education (from birth, preK to second grade, third to fifth grades, and middle school and high school). Overall, given the information presented in this chapter, it is critical to observe that Black home educators do not fit neatly into the same categories based on income level, family structure, or education level. Those within each grade level entry point may have some common characteristics—Black parents who decided to homeschool in grades 3–5, for example, stated that homeschool was not on their minds until specific interactions or incidents occurred—but Black home educators' motivations to homeschool also remain multifaceted. Across the entry points, issues of race, racism, school environment, home-school interactions, and parents' concerns for their children's academics, racial identity, and well-being drove their decisions in unique ways.

The remaining chapters address specific themes found in the narratives of Black home educators and present the diverse ways in which families represented each theme. The next chapter demonstrates the ways in which Black home educators identified homeschooling as a pathway toward healing.

CHAPTER 2

Black Home Education as a Pathway Toward Healing

Vanessa and Ben Harris made the decision to remove their children from their local public school due to dissatisfaction with the curriculum and instruction they received. Instead, they opted to participate in a co-op of predominantly White home educators whose beliefs about education aligned with their own. But problems soon developed. Vanessa explained,

> We were in a predominantly White homeschool co-op, but eventually our children began to feel like second-class citizens. They would find out that they didn't get invited to "Susan's" birthday party. Our children were not being allowed to go to people's houses, and children in the group were not being allowed to come to our house. The kids would tell us about what was going on. So, for us, we ended up starting our own group because we decided why work with something that's causing more harm to our children? We felt like if people really didn't want to be with us, then let's stop fighting that so we can get on with *our* homeschool. Just because it's all Black doesn't mean you don't have challenges and issues, but that [anti-Blackness] wasn't one of them any longer. So our children were able to feel more comfortable. We were able to *restore* and work on the fact that they were amazing people and that we didn't have to fight to be accepted because God had already accepted us.

People frequently ask some form of the question, "Why focus on Black home education? Isn't homeschooling just homeschooling?" Vanessa and Ben's experience offers a clear demonstration of why Black home education stands apart from other forms of homeschooling. In stating, "We can get on with *our* homeschool,"

Vanessa suggests a lack of belonging within the co-op. Moreover, Vanessa uses the word *restore* to describe an outcome of their homeschool practice. Restoration indicates a form of overcoming, or healing.

Regardless of when Black families began their home education practice, the narratives of Black home educators consistently point to a need to focus on healing in our educational practice. As seen in Vanessa and Ben's narrative, racial healing plays a significant role here, but this chapter examines other forms of healing that Black families perceived their home education afforded them as well. The chapter begins with a brief discussion of the theoretical and conceptual ideas undergirding notions of resistance as healing and then presents an overview of the study on homeschooling as healing, conducted in 2020. Next, I present findings on the multiple forms of healing that Black home educators experienced through their home education. Most importantly, this chapter presents ways in which educators in any setting could enact a mind-set of education as healing for all students based on Black home educators' experiences.

RESISTANCE AS HEALING

To be clear, homeschooling's use as a pathway toward healing does not imply that home education heals Black families. Instead, it has enabled Black families to experience movement toward healing in different aspects of their lives. In this study, resistance as healing is an ongoing, day-to-day process rather than a finite state of being. Artist and writer Okwui Okpokwasili has explained, "Healing as resistance allows us to open back up, to gather what has been scattered, to form new connections, and to affirm our lives together."[1] Black home educators' work and practices embody these ideas. Although the Black home education research literature has focused on resistance as avoiding and overcoming negative practices and policies, this chapter expands these conceptions of resistance to include resistance as healing. Black home educators often find themselves reflecting on their ancestral and family histories. They identify ways Black home education fosters their ability to reclaim historical practices and knowledge, and to create new connections with one another. Endarkened feminist epistemology, discussed in the introduction, frames this work as Black women's ways of knowing.

Further, resistance as healing suggests movement toward action and possibly some resolution. Scholars who focus on healing in Black communities indicate that our healing extends beyond racism, poverty, and sexism, and that healing is the "pathway to real justice," giving us the "capacity to restore our humanity and care for ourselves and others even during our fear" while moving us "confidently into a possible future."[2] By creating spaces for themselves and their children, Black parents foster a multifaceted healing that extends well beyond themselves.

RESEARCH OVERVIEW

In February 2020, I began a phenomenological study designed to explore Black home educators' perspectives on the ways in which Black home education had provided avenues toward healing, if at all. The twelve participating homeschool mothers shared their perspectives through interviews and three different Sister Circles. Sister Circles honor the ways of knowing, ways of socializing, and historical context of African American women.[3] The study's use of Sister Circle methodology provided Black women a unique form of support as part of the research process. Due to the onset of the COVID-19 pandemic, all interviews and Sister Circles were conducted using Zoom. The Sister Circles served to affirm and clarify thematic findings derived from line-by-line analysis of interview transcripts.

BLACK HOME EDUCATION AS HEALING

The study resulted in the identification of six, often overlapping, forms of healing facilitated by home educators' practice. First, Black home education provided racial healing. This refers to healing from prior experiences with anti-Blackness, internalized racism, or interactions with racism and prejudice experienced in school. Racial healing also includes the ability to counter and reduce negative impacts on children's racial self-identities. Second, Black home education provided mothers opportunities to heal from motherhood guilt and negative self-identity as mothers. Third, Black home education enabled Black children to heal academically. This went beyond correcting erroneous content to also include enabling Black children to see themselves as capable learners with a strong sense of self-efficacy and to develop an effective work ethic. Fourth, Black families also found healing through the process of homeschooling because it allowed them to strengthen family bonds, which also included the bonds between husbands and wives, thus enabling marriage healing. Black homeschooling has even fostered community-wide healing in some places. Finally, Black home education has provided intergenerational healing for Black families and communities. Black home educators frequently reflected on the strengths of their childhoods and the issues they wanted to "correct" or avoid as they raised their children, and home education enabled them to obtain these goals. Due to the overlapping nature of these six themes, this section will present data in the form of narratives exactly as Black mothers described perceptions of their healing through Black home education to demonstrate the interconnectedness of each form of healing, rather than trying to isolate the data within the six forms of healing. The findings on all six themes will be evident in this chapter and in the remaining chapters of the book.

Racial Healing and Intergenerational Healing

During Sister Circles, Black homeschool mothers bonded over challenges with their daughters' racialized experiences surrounding their hair in public school settings, which also conjured their own experiences related to their hair during childhood. Our shared experiences surrounding Black hair stemmed from other people's reactions to or desires to touch our hair. But they also brought up issues related to internalized self-hate in our wishes that our coils and curls could be more like the hair of the White children we encountered at school. For example, in response to another mother sharing about her child wanting to have her hair straightened all the time, Nancy, a married mother of five children, shared,

> I remember specifically, and I experienced the same when I was in public schools, . . . hair issues. I went to a predominantly White school in middle school, and I had long hair. My grandmother was a beautician, and she would do me and my cousins' hair the same way. She would press it because that was like the old-school way, to press it and hot comb it, and so my hair was long and thick. In my head, because I was attending school with all these White kids and their hair was long, and so I was doing that [*demonstrates swinging her long hair and stroking it*]. But my hair would get frizzy by the end of the day. Nobody was there to tell me, hey, [Nancy], you need to put that [hair] in a ponytail or something. As I got older, I would see my old yearbook pictures, and I'm like, why didn't anybody tell me? I'd take pictures and my hair is just everywhere, and nobody told me.

Reflecting on her children's school experiences, Nancy continued,

> So my older three children are girls, and they are the ones who went to public school. We went through that, where they wanted me to straighten their hair. They always wanted it straight. What can they do to make it straighter? Because I was just doing flat ironing it and, you know, we went through that where they

> didn't understand that their hair does not, it's not the same as their White counterparts'. And where we live, like [another Black home educator in the Sister Circle], our population is 4 percent African American, maybe 5 percent. So that even at church, that's who we see as well. I had to constantly reassure them, our hair is okay, it's okay. It's curly. That's how God made us. And I mean, that was a big, big struggle for us. Finally, they got used to it. They went through the ponytail stage.
>
> So for them it was the poof, the big afro poof. They would go to school with these big, huge proofs in their head and they would come home, "Mom, everybody wants to touch our hair because it's so different." Then my husband and I were like "nope" [*chuckles, others in Sister Circle smile*]. "You're not supposed to let people touch your hair. Their hands are dirty, your hair's clean," like we went through all of that. And that identity part at the elementary to middle school transition where you are trying to find yourself and you're trying to figure out just as a human, why am I growing like this, you know, and then you add on as, as an African American and why does my hair look like this? Why is my nose wider than everybody else's? And my lips are a little bit fuller? And so you have that added component. And in many cases, in public education, a lot of kids experience taunting behaviors regarding these differences because kids don't always know how to handle being different.

For generations, Black children have had to endure teasing and worse related to looking different or non-White. Some might dismiss this as child's play, but when play makes children want to be another race or be like another race, racism begins to be internalized. In her *Racial Healing Handbook*, scholar Anneliese Singh explains, "For people of color, internalized racism—the racialized and stereotyped ideas about their race they learn from the world and society—can result in a range of painful emotions and beliefs, stress, ambivalence or even hatred for their own culture, or a sense that life is harder for them for reasons they can't quite explain."[4] Even if unintentional, these interactions have dangerous, long-term implications for children of color if not addressed.

Yet, as shown in the vignette of Vanessa and Ben Harris, homeschooling in and of itself was not enough to bring about healing from internalized racism. Vanessa and Ben experienced racism within a predominantly White homeschool co-op. Such racialized experiences of prejudice or anti-Blackness, whether they take place in traditional school settings or homeschool co-ops, can damage Black children's sense of belonging and ultimately foster internalized racism. Beverly, who began homeschooling during the upper elementary years, joined the local homeschool co-op in her community, and she shared,

> When we first started homeschooling, we were the minority in a mostly Caucasian environment. And in time, our children began to feel, through just small . . . I don't know if you would call them microaggressions, but nothing overt. They just began to feel left out; not important. They would find out about birthday parties or events that their friends were invited to, but they were not. And the only ones who were not invited were people of color. And so we began to see that larger Caucasian culture, they were homeschooling in some ways to kind of create their own world and didn't really seem to want to allow us to be a part of it. So we decided if our kids were feeling like they weren't wanted, then it would be better for us to do our own group. Where we had other issues because we are dealing with people, but that [anti-Blackness/prejudice] was no longer an issue.

This experience resonated with Alana, who participated in the same Sister Circle. But her daughter attended a predominantly White Christian school, where one would hope the bond of a shared Christian faith would alleviate issues of racism. Alana shared,

> I know for me and my family, there's been a lot of healing that has taken place. It's not because of homeschooling, but homeschooling has played an important part for lots of reasons. One is because I could control the emotional pace of my family. When my daughter came out of the Christian private school and had dealt with some racism, she needed time to heal. We needed time to heal in very different ways. We needed some time with her in that healing process. Homeschooling allowed us to do just that. I was able to talk with her about my racial past and connect with her because one of the things that I was saying in my journal is that my experience was not her experience. I was from the North and there was a lot of desegregation in that area. I had White friends, then I had Black friends. I realized that I had put her in an environment where she was the only Black person, and she was experiencing some things that I don't think that I was totally aware of until I started seeing some signs. So homeschooling allowed us to walk that back and to fix some areas that we knew needed to be fixed. I just don't think that she would've been the same child if I had not homeschooled her.

Neither a predominantly White homeschool setting nor a predominantly White Christian school setting gave Black children an escape from the disparagement of anti-Blackness or racism. Prejudice, racism, and anti-Blackness exist even in settings where diverse families seemingly converge in educational aims for their children and in their faith. Indeed, recent scholarship has demonstrated that a predominantly White Christian school located in the Bible Belt served as "ground zero for experiences of anti-Black racism."[5] Black middle schoolers who attended the school described their educational setting as steeped in Whiteness through student-to-student and teacher-to-student interactions. In one exchange, a teacher said to a Black student, "You would be the first one to get shot in this class because you're Black."[6] Further, Black students in this Christian-based educational setting were aware of how the teachers' behaviors toward them influenced the students. "White teachers transmitted specific racial attitudes, while notably, ignoring the verbal assaults on Black students. Although teachers constantly surveilled the bodies, words and actions of Black students, white students acted and spoke freely, and with impunity. Teachers gave white students the grace of 'just being kids,' whereas Black students were chronically punished and pushed out of classrooms, even for the same behavioral infractions as their peers."[7] Thus, alignment among diverse groups of parents in terms of religious beliefs does not ensure that Black children will be treated as equals and provided with the education they need. But within predominantly Black homeschool spaces, Black mothers felt they could more fully access educational justice and enable racial healing for their children. This speaks to the importance of fostering affinity groups within diverse schools.

Black home education provided the time and space needed to respond to the broader issues of racism found within society as well. The murders of George Floyd and Breonna Taylor in the spring of 2020 spurred widespread protests in cities across the country, which prominently positioned police brutality in our Sister Circle. Alyssa, a married mother of a son who began homeschooling after he had been erroneously accused of assaulting a White student in his private school kindergarten class, explained,

> So if I think about our present situation with the prominence of killings of Black men by law enforcement and by White vigilantes and the protests and the unrest right now . . . what's been interesting is certainly we all know that as Black parents, we have controlled the amount of information and the timing of information we give to our children about policing, how to interact with the police, and what law enforcement means. In this very moment it has been important that we were *already* homeschoolers, and that we're homeschooling now, because it allows us to control what he [her son] sees for the most part, and what he hears. It allows us real time to talk with him about what he is seeing and hearing, and if he has emotions and feelings about that. I think if we had not been homeschooling,

> had he been in public school. . . . Because you might have had teachers or other students or other adults saying things, and sharing information that was either incorrect or hurtful or wrong or maybe helpful. I won't be overly skeptical, but the point is, particularly when you're dealing with very sensitive times in American society, and for us at this moment of police brutality—right?—homeschooling provides a chance to control the narrative our kids receive in positive ways and to control the amount of trauma they may experience from either classmates or teachers. So I think that's one way to either mitigate racial trauma or at least control the damage and retell the narrative. . . . *Restructure the narrative in a way that's positive and affirming for our children.* I think that's been *particularly important now.*

The decision to shut out society's influence on our children through home education might be considered overly protective or unrealistic and, for some, dangerous for the children.[8] But the protection that Alyssa refers to here is more of a buffering from a society that can be harsh and detrimental to Black people. Alyssa's comments suggest that the images and reports of Black citizens dying at the hands of police need to be discussed with Black children in ways that they can handle, not ignored.

Beverly, a veteran home educator of over twenty years and the wife of a career police officer, further explained,

> For me, it [media reports of police brutality] was a lot of stereotypes, a lot of statistical stereotypes that were not true. My husband is in law enforcement. So there is a lot that we bring to the table on that topic with his thirty-year career. There were a lot of things that we know just because of his work. Then there was a lot of things that we knew were more stereotypes. So I really needed to spend some time to heal personally because you can't teach out of anger because then you build another generation that's angry. They're angry about your experience instead of their own. So I knew that my children had to have their own experiences, and their own interpretation of those experiences as opposed to me bringing my pain forward. So I wanted to really spend some time for my own self to heal so that I could teach. Then once you have that time, then you can go into finding resources.

Combined, Alyssa's and Beverly's perspectives on approaches to racial healing through home education suggest a need for adults to consider the practice of critical media literacy with regard to news reports. There are always multiple perspectives on a topic, and teaching our children to understand this point can be quite effective, but we must make sure, as Beverly advises, that we have processed our anger and past hurts related to the topic first. Anger and pain can be passed down from one generation to the next if the time is not taken to reflect and heal.

Race-related news topics frequently show up directly in our classrooms. Susan who was homeschooling one of her four children at the time of the study, shed light on this fact:

> I will say that what happened in Central Park a couple of weeks ago with the birdwatcher Christian Cooper and Amy Cooper resonated with me. I read a thread on Twitter where an educator talked about how "Amy Cooper" shows up in the classroom. I just felt all kinds of emotions about that because my children have experienced the Amy Coopers in the classroom, be it in an educator or a student. I was processing, again, why we homeschool our current teenager. Then also thinking about, "Do we need to do this for our other children?" because I was thinking about the assault on Black children in the classroom. So this one child that we homeschool has felt that he has experienced that, and we had to have some conversations with him about this. We send him to school and then he comes home, and we're having to unlearn those things that were shared with him or things that were done to him in the classroom. I also think we're in a school district where "Amy Cooper" shows up, Amy Cooper–like behavior. We see that in the statistics. We see that in the statistics in terms of behavior and discipline as well as academic performance. So, for my son, he was in the discipline number, and it was at that point that we realized this is not going to be his narrative. He's not going to be a part of the statistics. For that, we need to remove him from this space. He needs to be in a space where learning is the focus and not necessarily the discipline piece, and the low [academic] performance of African American children in local schools. So that was our reasoning for wanting to homeschool.

Susan's remarks remind us that our racial healing requires us to create spaces for our children where they can be free from the stereotypes, low expectations, prejudice, and anti-Blackness that are applied to us whether they represent us or not. This common pursuit could be found among Black mothers across levels of educational attainment and socioeconomic status. Home education provided them the freedom to escape from negative statistics that fed into traditional educators' expectations and the freedom to avoid the school-to-prison pipeline that is tied so intimately with school discipline policies, which, as found in existing research on the state of Black education in traditional spaces, lead to discipline disproportionality.[9]

Motherhood Healing and Intergenerational Healing

The responsibility of guiding a child into adulthood in this challenging world can leave you riddled with self-doubt and guilt as a mother. Added to these challenges, Black mothers such as myself must raise our children in emotionally, physically, and psychologically hostile environments where the hostility is often projected by authorities such as police or educators. We increasingly observe needless tragedies in the death of Black children, which represents the incarnation of our deepest nightmares as Black mothers, as we are fearful "that we will not be able to adequately protect our children from or prepare them for a world that has to be convinced of their worth."[10] Our children are surrounded by messages conveying that they do not matter, they are not capable, and they are not beautiful, and as Black mothers we must work tirelessly to counter those messages daily. We must do so without breaking their spirits or coddling them. It is a balancing act. Black mothers approach these issues differently. How do you, or should you, explain to your Black children that even though Jim Crow has legally ended, we are still not free?

Akilah Richards, author of *Raising Free People*, shared her experiences as a Black unschooling educator.[11] Unschooling is an approach to home education that centers children, their interests, and natural curiosity in the instructional practice. As a mother and unschooling educator, Richards writes about the dissonance she experienced in raising her children to use their voices for themselves compared with how she was raised as a Black child. Ultimately, Richards expands our understanding of unschooling by applying it to her parenting and the relationship she has developed with her daughters. In describing their journey, Richards relates spankings to the beatings African slaves received during slavery, and she identifies the need to decolonize childhood. For me, as someone who interpreted the Holy Bible's scripture stating, "Spare the rod, spoil the child," found in Proverbs 13:24 as meaning parents should spank their children for correction, Richards's connection of spanking to slavery presented a huge moment of pausing and reflecting for me. Might the scriptures refer to something other than spanking children? Should children be raised to fear their parents? Further, how do home educators integrate the role of teacher into their motherhood challenges, and what possibilities for healing develop as a result?

In our Sister Circles, we shared in the joys and blessings of being mothers. But we also talked about the challenges of being Black mothers in a society that does not value Blackness. Jessica, a single mother of two children who had been homeschooling for seven years, shared with a circle of four Black home educators,

> When I learned that I was going to have a girl, I cried. I did not want to have a girl. I remember literally walking out of the doctor's office, sitting in the hallway, and having a complete meltdown. The reason was because I have such a tumultuous relationship with my own mother that I was just terrified of the same thing . . . of repeating the dynamics between my mother and I, being very . . . not black and white, but just murky. Like there's so many amazing things that my mother did to raise me. So much sacrifice and so many ways she showed love. But in other ways, I did not feel loved by her, but I felt abandoned by her and all these different things. I couldn't quite reconcile those feelings. Frankly, I'm still trying to reconcile them.

Jessica continued,

> I didn't ever want my daughter to grow up having those same conflicts that I had. Growing up I had a lot of White friends and their relationships with their moms was always like friends. Then I would come home, and my mom was like, "I'm the mother!" "Don't talk back to me," or "I'll knock you into next week." I just thought that the positive mother-daughter relationship was a White thing and I longed for that. So maybe that was a form of internalizing wanting some form of Whiteness in my life. But when I looked around to other Black families it was kinda the Black mama is a Black mama. So I didn't want my daughter to grow up being afraid of me and like she couldn't talk to me like I did. So I was so intentional not to repeat certain things that I felt were damaging to me. That became my focus in homeschooling. Like I couldn't just relax into motherhood. I'd always say to myself, "I'm not gonna do that. I'm not going to do this, and I'm not going to say it this way." So homeschooling has made me look. . . . It's like a mirror. It's been really, really, really hard. How do you navigate a mother-daughter relationship when you didn't grow up with the tools to do so? So not only have I been homeschooling, but I've also been trying to find tools to help with the relationship piece.

For Jessica, homeschooling spurred a self-reflection process that encouraged intergenerational healing related to her childhood hurts and her beliefs about motherhood. While giving birth to her daughter conjured fears of motherhood for Jessica, serving as her daughter's educator provided the impetus to work through unresolved issues in her relationship with her own mother. Home education typically requires mothers to spend all day with their children, and this increased time demands mother-child interaction, communication, and relationship building. Notably, even after seven years of homeschooling, Jessica shared that she continued to work on building a relationship with her daughter, indicating that healing takes time and is an ongoing process.

Jessica's vulnerability led other participants in the circle to share their experiences with home education as a vehicle for healing related to fears and concerns about motherhood. Annise, a widowed home educator, expressed her present challenges with being a mother and home educator of her six-year-old son. She shared,

> For me, I have the mom guilt, but I'm widowed. My husband passed away; August will make two years. And so I'm still working all of that out. Especially for him because he didn't get to spend that much time with him [his father] and he had four years practically. So for me it adds that dynamic to it. Regarding the healing, I think our relationship is going to change because I was home with him for two and half years before my husband passed, and then I went to work shortly after, and I recently resigned so I'm back home full time again. But for two and half years he was in someone else's care [her son attended a public school during this time]. And I saw his personality change and behaviors changed and, yes, so I'm trying to get him back to where he was, where he had me around all the time. So that's the healing that I'm looking for. I'm not trying to force too much structure on him right away because I think what we did initially worked. He did well academically. I think I just need to heal that time he spent in someone else's care. The thing is, you don't know who's, see . . . I put him in someone else's care. Right? I don't know who you are [meaning her son's teachers], what you do when you are home. I don't know what your intentions are for my child.

While her son attended public school, she observed him developing self-hate due to his Black skin. Recall Annise's account, presented in chapter 1, of how he came home from school one day and frantically washed his hands. When she asked him why, he told her he was trying to wash the Black off. Something or someone in her son's school made him hate himself because of his race. This contributed to the guilt she felt as a mother. In her mind, it would not have happened if she had been home with him. She further explained,

> So my focus is for him to know himself, and that's focusing on our culture. What African, Caribbean, African American, the whole thing, so that he understands who he is, because that's the difference I see with him and my other three children. They know who they are and they're unshakable when it comes to that. There's no excuse for who they are. And then on top of that, being a single

> mother, trying to figure out who I am, how to live as a single parent now, and just all of that.

Annise believes home education serves as a way of restoring her son's racial and cultural self-identity to a positive framing as a way of undoing what he had inaccurately learned about his Blackness while in school. In comparison, when Annise describes her older children's sense of their cultural and racial identities, she poignantly uses the word *unshakable*, as in unwavering and resolute. Annise's older children had been educated in the Virgin Islands, their native homeland and presumably a space where their racial and cultural identities were highly valued.

Black home educators also identified ways in which home education served as a path toward healing for them as women. Alana, a home educator and homeschool leader with more than twenty years of experience, shared,

> Homeschool was a place of inner healing for me. I thought I was doing this for my children, and I learned so much about [Alana]. The good, the bad, and the ugly. But the person that I became after we raised those three children up, I do not think I would be that woman if I had not homeschooled for that time. Because there's nothing that uncovers things like being with your children 24/7, nothing. I learned that I was an angry woman. I learned that I disciplined my children based on other people's faces. I learned that it was more important what other people thought than what my family thought. I learned that I was prejudiced, and that my oldest daughter, because she was very strong academically, was supposed to be the standard. And anybody else *was less than*. And I actually, without knowing it, told them that. And so I had to repent and ask for forgiveness for comparing because I did not honor the way that my other children had been created. And so I had to find the beauty of slow, and find out that God has purpose for everything, and that I had to honor it before the child could be able to honor it and see it. And as I began to honor it, I was able to help them to see their beauty. And in our culture, parents do not, at least my growing up, parents don't apologize. Okay? So to be able to humble myself to the place where I not only learned how to apologize but I learned how to apologize without exception—"I'm sorry, but if you had to . . ." The buts had to go; it was, "Mommy is wrong. Can you please forgive me? And I need you to know I intend to never do that again."

Alana's vulnerability demonstrates, once again, our need to consider intergenerational healing in our motherhood practices. But she also demonstrates that homeschooling enabled her to reframe her perspective on motherhood and fostered humility in motherhood. It revealed that she was unintentionally inflicting pain on her children by comparing them with the oldest child. Homeschooling enabled her to see her own anger so that she could begin to interrogate it. These revelations had an impact on her discipline practice, her priorities, and the relationship she had with her children.

As a home educator with twenty-plus years of experience, Alana also served as a home education leader in her community and across the country. As a homeschool leader she helped guide other parents in their home education practices. She explained that she shared what she learned about herself in her homeschool practice as part of her training of new home educators. (We will explore more of Alana's role as a homeschool leader in chapter 6.) Based on her Christian beliefs, she described the process of developing her home education practice as a spiritual one. She explained,

> No one else would've known. It was private, it was hidden. I never showed it in public, but it was something inside that said, "That's not okay. And you need to do better, and you can do better." Because I realized that I'm responsible. I'm a steward. I've been given a gift [her children]. They don't belong to me. And at the end of the day, I'm going to be judged on how I do this. And that's homeschool. It's not just academics. It's so much more than that. In fact, what I teach is, there are foundational things about inner, about relating to one another, about loving, about emotional healing, about spiritual maturity that are our foundation. When we build those things first, the homeschool is almost, it just naturally grows out of that. But if you are a mom and you're not willing to acknowledge that you need to grow emotionally or grow spiritually, you're only going to be able to give your child but so much.

Alana's descriptions of the healing process resonated with Susan in the Sister Circle. Susan responded,

> So, I want to piggyback on that. When I tell people I homeschool, because most people, parents I know, do not homeschool. . . . They sort of look at me in amazement and they say, literally, "I could never do that. I could never spend that much time with my children. I could never be both parent or mother, sometimes father, and teacher." And I think, to [Alana's] point, it's the continually being in the same space with your child that forces human growth. Children do it, I think, a lot quicker than adults because children will say what's on their mind. They will tell you if you have done something wrong. They will tell you that what you are asking or demanding is not fair or appropriate or nice or what they want to do. And when that happens, you learn. You have a choice to make about how you're

> going to respond. And I think to the extent that you are connected to your children, or want to relate with your children, just as human beings, and you're willing to learn from them while you are also trying to help them grow, then there's a lot of opportunity for learning about yourself, for healing yourself. And so, I think just generally, I would echo that it's been a learning process, a growth process, whether it's my own issues, or intergenerational issues, or mothering issues, or thinking about even how I relate to my husband versus how I relate to my son. Right?

This exchange between Alana and Susan excites me because it says so much about parenting and motherhood that we only discuss in sacred safe places, which means Black home educators experienced the Sister Circle precisely as it was intended to be experienced even though it was a digital Zoom space. These home educators broke down the healing process within their homeschool practices. Their willingness to listen to their children's critique or commentary about their homeschool practice played a central role in their growth as home educators, mothers, and women. Healing depended on home educators' willingness to listen to their children and take their complaints, dispositions, and suggestions seriously. How often do we really listen to students' feedback on our instruction as educators?

The extended time that home educators have with their children provides an opportunity for parents to get to know their children as learners and, more importantly, as people. In a previous publication, I wrote about a single Black home educator who had to first figure out whether she liked her child because she had never before spent as much time with her daily![12] Like Alana and Susan, this home educator found herself getting to know her child in a new way, with greater depth. Susan qualifies her remarks about the connectedness between parents and their children with "the extent" that they connected and the degree to which they wanted "to relate with" them. This indicates that having the extra time through home education is not enough. Parents who choose to be home educators must intentionally seek connectedness with their children. Finally, the strength of Black home educators' healing depended on their willingness to reflect on their own shortcomings to the point of being vulnerable and willing to change.

Overall, intergenerational healing served as a common factor across racial healing and motherhood healing as well. When Black mothers homeschool, they reflect on things they were taught or experienced in their childhoods. We saw how the racial harm that occurs in school can contribute to mothers' guilt for not being able to prevent such hurt, and how homeschooling helps mothers to begin to process and remedy the situation.

Educational justice for Black parents and children enables teaching and learning practices in which we are free to create space and time for healing. Here homeschooling provides the "freedom to be and to become" with the flexibility to recognize, acknowledge, and address racialized harm, which is particularly poignant given the current state of society as states seek to scrub diversity, equity, and inclusion language from teaching standards.[13] To secure educational justice for Black children through home education, adults must be willing to engage in self-reflection, and inner-child work, in order to understand our past hurts so they can be reconciled in the present. The healing that stems from Black home education also tends to occur within the spaces Black families create for themselves. The next section considers how what we have gleaned from Black home educators' perspectives on home education as a pathway toward healing can be applied to educational practice in traditional schools.

HEALING IMPLICATIONS FOR EDUCATIONAL SPACES

When I was a teacher in the 1990s, renowned educator Marva Collins came to speak to the teachers in my school district. In her talk, she repeatedly said, "I cannot tell you what to do; I am telling you what I would do." Many of my colleagues did not understand what she was saying to us. They felt as though they had not learned anything from her. But I left that space feeling empowered. I understood that what she was willing to do was really what needed to be done on behalf of children and did not necessarily fall within the confines of what administration or even our teachers' union would have us do. This is the spirit in which I approach this section on implications. To be an effective teacher, children must come first, not test scores or standards.

Affinity Groups

Black home educators clearly identified the need to create spaces of their own to be able to begin to heal from racism and anti-Black experiences. To me, this calls us all to consider how we might employ affinity groups in traditional learning spaces. Affinity groups are created when we assemble people based on a particular characteristic such as gender or race.[14] Like affinity groups, predominantly Black homeschool spaces became sources of support and encouragement. Black home educators did not say their Black-led co-op spaces were perfect. But the spaces they created did not have anti-Blackness to contend with, unlike other spaces they encountered, even Christian spaces. Similarly, affinity groups have been used successfully in classrooms and on behalf of teachers in the spirit of culturally relevant processes. Affinity groups have also been used as a counseling or mediation method. They serve as a coping mechanism that helps Black students release and process the challenges of being an ethnic minority within school and outside it, while also being affirmed in their Blackness.[15] Unfortunately, given the political nature of education, school administrations have begun to disregard and even ban formal race-based affinity groups and programs.

Yet affinity groups can also be informal or even impromptu. As an example, one year when I was teaching fourth grade, I had two high-spirited Black female students with very strong personalities who clashed with each other constantly. I knew I had to do something, but what? Back then I could not have articulated the precise desire not to engage in spirit murdering, but I did know they would need their vivacious spirits to be successful in the future and that their spunk represented a deep part of who they were as human beings. This was something that must remain intact. But how could I get them to pull together? When their seeming hatred of each other had come to a boiling point, I decided to invite both young ladies to have lunch with me. During this lunch, I focused on what the three of us had in common as Black females. I told them that, for all we knew, we could all be descendants of royalty in Africa. I discussed our strengths and how we need those strengths inside and beyond our classroom, but that we should not be fighting each other because there is greater strength if we are united. Life in our classroom changed. The young ladies pulled together. Twelve years later, one of those young ladies tracked me down, even though I had left the state and become a professor almost one thousand miles away from our home state of Connecticut, and she wrote me an email. It said,

> Hello Professor Smith,
> I don't know if you remember me, but you were my first black female teacher, at [school in Connecticut] in 1998. My name is [Maya (pseudonym)], and I was one of the few black female students in the class, I think there were only five. I know you are probably wondering why I am writing you, if I were you, I would probably be thinking the

> same thing. For many years now I wanted to say thank you for your strong, empowering, and motivating words! I didn't quite understand the lesson back then, but I fully comprehend it now. The story begins with me and [a fellow classmate] calling me the B word during an argument in the reading area. You had lunch with us in the classroom, one on each side of you and you told us to love each other. You told us as black females we must learn to respect ourselves, and if we don't, no one will. You told us how the world will constantly doubt us, expect too much from us, and never sympathize for us. Your words have been in my heart for twelve years now; you are the one who sparked the flame of change in my soul. For as far as I can remember I have been heavily involved in community service, being an advocate for the youth, and using my voice to speak for those who have been oppressed. I have been the president of [her university's] collegiate chapter of the NAACP, a Resident Advisor, a tutor, a mentor, a counselor, a sister, and most important of them all a positive role model. As I walked across the stage this past May receiving my Bachelor's degree, I couldn't help but think of the people who aided me to get where I am today. You are on the top of the list; because you taught me at the youngest age that you can do anything once you put your mind to it. I cannot say thank you enough, as I write this email my eyes are swelling with tears that I was fortunate enough to have someone who impacted my life so much. Not many individuals get that chance, that's how I know that God truly has blessed me. . . . Thank you for going outside of the box, out on limb, and changing my life.

My eyes well up every time I think about this email and how taking the time to talk with these young ladies had such a huge impact on this woman. She did not fully understand it at the time, but because I took the time to talk and to listen, this student held on to my words until they became fully comprehendible. In another part of the email, my former student says that she wants to use her education to "reconstruct policies to *free* His children from the various institutions that they have been place[d] in." The investment of that twenty-five-minute lunchtime resulted in the development of a leader and change agent working on behalf of children and youth.

To be clear, I had no prior training in how to deal with this situation. I approached it as an impromptu affinity group of Black females and with a great deal of sincere care for the two human beings who were my charges for the school year. I instinctively recognized these students' verve, high-spiritedness, and curiosity as a strength, not a problem. In a school culture or with an educational philosophy that prioritizes controlling and surveilling students' bodies and voices, we will be quite challenged to value students who voice their opinions, call out loud, and ignore the "stay in your seat" or "raise your and wait to be called on" type of classroom policies.

What if I had been a different race or gender from these two students? Or a teacher of any race who could only see these students as worrisome instead of recognizing the potential they held? Many educators would only see these young ladies' interactions as a behavior problem. But regardless of a teacher's racial or ethnic identity, they should be able to find some common ground between these ladies by drawing on observations of who they are as learners and as human beings. The conversation could be a sharing of the teacher's observations regarding their strengths and concern for the missed opportunities of working together. Children of color often have "play" moms, dads, and aunties (fictive kinfolk) in the school building or in the community whom we can partner with to bring about positive change or the reframing of students' mind-sets. The possible solutions offered by forming affinity spaces are endless. The point here would be to tap into your available sources and knowledge to guide the students toward collaboration or connection by creating a space where they can see their common ground and heal any past hurts. As educators, we must care enough to take the time to do something different.

Educator Self-Reflection and Self-Efficacy

Black home education mothers engaged in deep self-reflection as participants in the Sister Circle methodology and when they were interviewed in multiphase interviews. In some cases, they may have realized and recognized their healing through participation in the Sister Circles. Renowned psychologist Joy Harden Bradford explains that when Black women form sisterhood, we are seen, we are supported, we gain an increased understanding of ourselves, and we can soften toward or trust others more easily.[16] This aligns with endarkened feminist epistemologies, which posit, "Only within the context of community does the individual appear."[17] The Sister Circle promoted self-reflection. The critical role of self-reflection can be seen when reading across the principles and tenets of multicultural education, culturally relevant pedagogy, culturally responsive pedagogy, and similar approaches, which urge us to begin with self-reflection, including identifying our own biases. Such reflection takes time and requires safe spaces if its insights are to be shared. As a teacher educator, I have often wondered, Where in our program do we allow for such extensive reflection? To be sure, there are some reflective activities embedded throughout our courses, but is this enough? I believe that as educators, self-reflection is a practice that we must develop and sustain over the course of our careers, because it has the potential to be the most influential form of professional development that we can engage in.

What types of truly safe spaces exist for educators to engage in collaborative self-reflection that could lead to transformation and the reframing of our teacher practice? For example, engaging in a reading circle with other educators can sometimes promote such opportunities for self-reflection. One of the most transformational self-reflection experiences I have ever had was during a professional development training in teacher self-efficacy while I was teaching second grade in Stamford, Connecticut.

The Self-Efficacy Institute out of Boston came to work with us during a week one summer, and at least 90 percent of the school staff participated. Most of us attended the first self-efficacy session wearing pins we had received at a recent end-of-the-year celebration. The small apple-shaped pins had "All Children Can Learn" printed on them. Our self-efficacy trainer intuitively used those pins to hold us accountable in applying the content she was presenting to our teacher practice. She did this by simply asking us, "What does 'All Children Can Learn' look like in your classroom?" That week, we openly shared our triumphs in realizing all children can learn, but more importantly, we began sharing about the times when we failed to realize the vision of all children learning in our classroom. As an example, we held one another responsible for talking about our students in generative ways. When someone positioned their students in disparaging ways by saying, "These kids can't . . . ," or "won't . . . ," or "don't . . . ," teacher colleagues would disrupt this negative talk and remind the teacher, "All children can learn," so what is getting in the way of your students' learning? Saying "these kids" enables a lack of ownership over our responsibility for student learning, which signals a need to reflect on our self-efficacy related to our ability to teach all students. Focusing on what our students cannot do will not lead us toward resolution of the issues. A more effective conversation would start by asking, What can the students do related to the learning challenge or concept? What might be preventing the children from learning this concept? What resources do I have to address those possible barriers? Who else might be able to support these students' learning?

Though I had never heard of Brené Brown at the time, thinking about this period in my career, I now realize we had tapped into what Brown refers to as the "power of vulnerability."[18] We left that weeklong training with a new mind-set regarding the potential impact of our instruction even among those students who encounter challenges in learning. Moreover, we continued to wear our "All Children Can Learn" pins with new meaning. We could now tell anyone how we applied this motto to our own instruction, and we held each other accountable for doing so. I felt bad for the few faculty who had missed this critical experience! If education is going to have a healing component, then teachers must collaborate and share responsibility for children's learning. We must encourage self-reflection in an authentically vulnerable way.

Responding to National and Global Traumas

Unlike homeschooled children, students who attend traditional schools may not have the space and time needed to fully process local, national, and world events. As I write this, wars are raging in multiple places around the world, and the US involvement is highly political, which can produce anxiety. Nationally, there are factions that are pushing for a color-blind curriculum or a whitewashed version of history in our curriculum. Our country cannot find common ground on ways to address gun violence and crime. We are experiencing inflation and more. I wonder to what extent these real-life issues have been taken up in classrooms. Do we just continue to teach the prescribed district curriculum and ignore the happenings around the world and here at home?

On January 7, 2021, the day after the attack on our nation's capital, as a teacher educator I reached out to a few of my former students who were now teaching in classrooms to see how things were going. I did this because I remembered what it was like to teach fourth grade the day after the Columbine massacre in 1999. I could not teach, but I knew I had to let my students talk through the fears and concerns they had. Most stated that they felt safe in elementary school but had fears of going to middle and high school. I was able to get a guidance counselor to come into our classroom that day to help. But I had to call some parents that evening to let them know about our day. My students needed space to process what they had seen and heard in the news. So I wondered how children were doing after the January 6 Capitol insurrection.

One former student broke down in tears as he shared what January 7 was like for him and his students. He was teaching fifth grade and his classroom consisted primarily of Black and Brown students. His students were human beings who had only been on the planet for ten or eleven years. Yet when the Pledge of Allegiance came on that morning, there was a different response. One student said, "Hell no, I'm not saying that s——." Thankfully, her teacher, my former student, had the presence of mind to say, "You don't have to, but can we talk about it?" As he allowed them to voice their concerns, it became clear that these young children knew more than most adults would imagine. They understood what they saw and heard on television the evening before. White people tried to take over the Capitol and almost got away with it. More importantly, though, these children knew that had the Capitol attackers been Black or Brown, it would have been a bloodbath. They had internalized the implications of this reality: "Why should I do well in school in a country that hates me because of my skin color? What's the point?"

We had to do something. I had no idea what that something could be. I asked my teacher educator colleagues to meet to share what I had learned about our former student's fifth graders' response to January 6 and shortly after that meeting, the Righteous Rage Virtual Art Studio (RRVAS) was birthed. RRVAS was a collaboration between the fifth-grade teacher, the school counselor, a faculty member who had been embedded in the school when these fifth graders were in younger grades, a faculty member who was an artist, several local artists in the community, the children, and me. We used language and art to express anger, fears, and joy. The art was therapeutic for the adults and the children. The guidance counselor modeled ways to express our feelings with words. For all the adults and the children who participated in RRVAS, we had to invest extra time and energy beyond our regular school and workloads. Time is such a precious commodity. We all have a limited amount each day. But we all agreed that the most important thing we did during that time was to show the children that they matter to us. How do you show your students that they matter to you? Students in schools around the world needs spaces like RRVAS.

CHAPTER 3

Black Home Educator Folk Pedagogy as Putting Children First

If she [my daughter] is tired and gets up and she's, like, kind of antsy or not able to focus, I find the day goes better if I say, "You know what—let's put our pencils down and go for a walk." And we go for a walk and sometimes that's the *best* learning! We found a shell, a skeleton, and it was great! We saw mushrooms and we looked at those and we came back home, and she wrote in her journal what she found. She asked, "What kind of mushroom is that?" "Well, let's look it up." And we'll go and look up something about the mushroom and she'll go, "No, that's the cap." One neighbor was pretty good with mushrooms—sometimes I don't know which ones are poisonous or not—so we cut one, dissected one. You know, this is all in a day that started as a rough day. It turned out to be so much better after that walk.

—Hope, home educator to two children

This is from the book I found in the library on unschooling. You know how you can just look at something and start investigating? Do you know what I mean? You find just from that one investigation you can cover so many subjects. It's amazing! I mean, I remember our very first homeschool day to this day and basically, we went for a walk. We decided to just look at nature. We talked about the trees and why some of them are still green at this time of the year. And stuff like that. We came across grass, and he [my son] asked, "Why was the grass brown?" That launched our investigation and we learned that there are over two hundred types of grass!

—Yolanda, home educator to one of her two sons

Whether we are teachers or parents, what we believe about how people learn, how we conceive of an educator's role in the learning process, and what we think about our students guide how we will approach our teaching. Noted scholar Jerome Bruner ascribes this to folk pedagogy. He explains, "Watch any mother, any teacher, even any babysitter with a child and you'll be struck by how much of what they do is steered by notions of 'what children's minds are like and how to help them learn,' even though they may not be able to verbalize their pedagogical principles."[1] Although the Black home educators interviewed varied a great deal in their approach to teaching and learning, they demonstrated a shared belief in placing children at the center of their pedagogical decision-making. Coincidentally, by placing children first, such Black home educators are also embodying the theories of educational thinkers of the Progressive Era such as John Dewey, Lev Vygotsky, and others associated with constructivism, experiential learning, and more. Admittedly, home educators rarely acknowledged these pedagogues in educational theory, but teacher education programs do. What happens within schools today in terms of policy and practice appears to contrast with these values. Some scholars have even critiqued Progressive Era approaches to teaching and learning as not suitable for ethnic-minority children. Yet Black homeschool children thrive with these practices.

In the vignettes that open this chapter, Hope and Yolanda provide examples of how the Black home educators in my research placed children first through a broad range of teaching strategies, from paying attention to children's energy levels and temperaments to basing instruction on the questions children ask naturally. These snippets of data provide insight into Black home educators' folk pedagogy. Hope's home education practice placed children first by paying attention to her daughter's ability to focus. As a home educator, she believed she could not effectively teach, nor could her daughter learn, if she was fidgety and unable to focus. Hope also believed that learning could occur anywhere and that as an educator she would need to be flexible enough to align her instruction to her daughter's needs rather than sticking with her plans for the day. She valued flexibility in her instruction and appreciated nature as a meaningful learning context. Finally, Hope's instructional approach valued collaborating with available resources such as her neighbor as partners in her teaching.

Similarly, Yolanda's approach to teaching and learning did not require rigid lesson plans. Instead, guided by a book she had read, her homeschool instruction began with a walk and focused on a question her son had asked, "Why is the grass brown?" In the process of exploring answers to this question, Yolanda's son learned how to learn, how to research answers to his own questions. Yolanda's approach to home education demonstrated her belief that she did not have to know all the answers as the teacher and, instead, she could learn with her child. She also collaborated with community members. Both Hope's and Yolanda's folk pedagogy focused on putting their children first in their learning, though in slightly different ways.

Placing children first remained a primary feature of Black home educators' teaching even though they varied in their approaches to teaching and learning. Black home educators shared a variety of factors that inspired them to place children at the center of their own learning, including parents' own natural instincts, cultural beliefs, other home educators, and a few educational philosophers. This chapter unpacks Black home educators' folk pedagogy related to putting children first in their education. Though references to educational philosophers and thinkers were limited among Black home educators, they were greatly influenced by the work of Charlotte Mason and John Holt, as well as by the Waldorf approach and the Montessori method.

In this chapter, I present a comparison of these educational philosophies to highlight the diverse interpretations of what it means to put children first in teaching and learning. Next, I present data from my Black home education research to demonstrate additional aspects of Black home educators' folk pedagogy related to putting children first and how this feature of their folk pedagogy led to transformational academic healing and transformed Black children's mind-sets to allow them to see themselves as learners. Finally, the chapter ends with suggested strategies to implement a children-first approach to teaching in traditional schools, even within the constraints of high-stakes testing.

EDUCATIONAL PHILOSOPHIES CITED BY BLACK HOME EDUCATORS

Over the course of my seventeen years interacting with Black home educators, four educational philosophies have stood out as key influences. In this section, I provide a brief overview of each of these philosophies and an exemplar of how Black home educators talked about them. The philosophies are discussed in chronological order of their development in educational history. Table 3.1 provides an

TABLE 3.1 Comparison of philosophies cited by Black home educators for putting children first

	Charlotte Mason (1895)	*Montessori method (1907)*	*Waldorf approach (1919)*	*John Holt (1960)*
Primary principle of learning	• Liberal arts education • Real-life experiences • Knowledge of concepts and ideas, not memorization	• Child-centered, child-authored learning • Focus on independence, curiosity, and inner discipline	• Holistic education, emphasizing the development of the whole child—mind, body, and spirit	• Child-centered learning • Natural curiosity • Hands-on instruction
Assessment/ testing	Discourages formal testing in the early years and focused on qualitative assessments through narration and discussions	Authentic assessment methods of observation, checklists, and portfolios	Discourages formal testing, focused on qualitative assessment, portfolios, narration, and discussion	Criticizes traditional testing and grading systems, believing they hindered true understanding and love of learning
Curriculum approach	Encouraged a rich curriculum including literature, the arts, and nature study	Self-directed activities of children's choosing in mixed age groups, hands on	An arts-integrated curriculum with a strong emphasis on creativity, imagination, and play as well as content subject area coursework	Emphasizes experiential and self-directed learning
Role of the teacher	A guide and mentor, introducing children to a broad range of knowledge through literature and experiences	Sets up the classroom environment for learning and observes children	A guide and facilitator, fostering a warm and creative learning environment	A facilitator, guiding children in their learning journeys, allowing for self-direction

Note: This chart was created with partial support from Claude.ai.

overview of each philosophy's primary principle of learning, its stance on assessment, its curriculum approach, and the role of the teacher within it.

Charlotte Mason

Charlotte Mason was an English educator who established the House of Education in 1895 in England. Unlike most of her contemporaries, Mason believed that "all children were 'hungry for knowledge' and wanted to know—about everything."[2] Steeped in Christianity, she further posited, "Children are born persons."[3] Her educational philosophy included a holistic approach to a liberal arts education with an emphasis on real-life experiences. The Charlotte Mason approach to teaching and learning places teachers in the position of facilitators or guides rather than sole providers of knowledge.[4] Teachers use observation, narratives, and other holistic and authentic strategies to evaluate student progress.

Portia, a home education veteran of over ten years and follower of the Charlotte Mason method, explained,

> She [Mason] believed that narration was more important than a lot of tests because a child can take a test on Friday and take the same test on Monday and wouldn't know it. She believed that narration, meaning that the child writes a little paragraph about what they read, is long-term learning more so than a test because you're engaging your long-term memory by writing something out as opposed to tests, which tend to be for short-term memory. So that's why she didn't believe in a whole lot of tests. I have them narrate. My fourth grader gave me oral narrations. But my sixth-grade one gives oral narration too, and I'm like, okay, now it's time for you to write! [*Laughter*] My eighth grader wanted to give oral narratives too, and I'm like, no, now you really have to write too. I find that even if I don't look at it again, when you write it, you maintain a lot more of the information by writing it out. So I do that.

Portia became interested in the Charlotte Mason approach when she learned about it because it reminded her of the Waldorf method, which her sons began their education journey in and she had fully embraced. Like most home educators, Portia learned about the Charlotte Mason approach from other homeschool parents and then researched it on her own. Portia shared,

> I came across the Charlotte Mason approach in my research preparing to homeschool my boys. Now, Charlotte Mason was an educator back in England and she

> was the first to push for the homeschool movement. She was Christian and she grew up in England, where if you didn't have money you didn't go to school. So there were a ton of kids that could not go to school because they didn't have money. So she said, "Why should education be just for people with money?" She came up with a program that parents could teach their children at home. I came across her information on the internet, and I read a lot about her. I really liked her approach because she believed that children's minds are just full of things and the more you fill them, the more rounded and cultured they become. So she believed in having the children study artists, composers, and British and American history. So that's the first curriculum that I used. It was classical. We would read a lot of good books and engage their minds. You know, open up their minds to different things. So I used her because I read a lot about classical education, and like the Waldorf approach, they didn't use textbooks. Textbooks are things that textbook companies want your child to know. That's not necessarily what children *should* know. Let them read regular books written during the Civil War. Like my son has read *Abigail Adams: Witness to a Revolution*, with her back-and-forth to John Adams about the Revolutionary War. She had another perspective about the war. So let them learn about it through her perspective. Kids can get a different understanding. These companies are rewriting history as far as I'm concerned. They are taking things out and adding things and you are not getting the true history. So we study British history, we study about the kings, and we also study about American history. So she just believed in engaging the child and so much. You can't give them too much. Their appetites should be just well rounded and a lot of different books to get them thinking.

Portia gave numerous examples of how she applied the Charlotte Mason classical education approach in her home education practice. In this example of teaching about the Revolutionary War, I noticed the freedom Portia's sons gained by learning multiple perspectives on the war instead of the primarily White, male-dominant version frequently taught in public schools. This reminded me of Ronald Takaki's *A Different Mirror: A History of Multicultural America* and the accompanying version for children, both of which provide readers with the history of how many different ethnic groups contributed to the making of America.[5] Portia wanted her sons to know true history. True history has multiple perspectives, not just one version.

Currently the United States seems to have taken a step backward regarding teaching history. We increasingly hear about the banning of books, and there is a movement toward removal of words such as *diversity*, *inclusion*, and *equity* from our standards.[6] Moreover, forces are at work to remove diverse perspectives of our

American history from the curriculum.[7] But Mason and Portia suggest that children and youth should have the freedom to form their own understandings as they learn. In this way, students will garner more interest and lasting meaning from what they learn. Furthermore, Mason's approach demonstrates that our students are capable of learning much more than we expect of them.

Montessori Method

Started in 1907 by Maria Montessori, this method of teaching and learning positions children as the "authors" of their learning.[8] The Montessori method is based on self-directed learning within a somewhat controlled environment. Classrooms usually consist of mixed age groups. Teachers create classrooms to encourage students' curiosity, independence, and inner discipline and then track student progress through observations and based on age-appropriate guidelines.[9] Teacher observations and their use of checklists and portfolios provide assessment of student progress.

Although information on the Montessori method is proprietarily managed, Black home educators found resources that they could use to inform their homeschool practice. As an example, Magnolia, a married home educator for her son and daughter, shared,

> I started reading about homeschool before we placed her [daughter] in a school, so I was familiar with the different curriculums. I was also familiar with the Montessori philosophy, which I thought fit more with her [daughter's] type of learning style. And we knew that she needed the type of learning where she's moving around constantly and not sitting down. Paper and pencil—and then plus she told us that it was boring at the school when she was there because all they do all day is sit down and they must be quiet.

Her husband added, "We had found this all-Black Montessori school. But they charged about $630 a month and we can't afford that because it would have been $1,260 with our second child." Magnolia and her husband had also checked out books from the public library on how to practice Montessori in the home. For this family, the active engagement found in the Montessori method aligned with the parents' observations of their oldest child's learning style but conflicted with the more restrictive, regimented approach to teaching and learning found in their locally assigned public school. They believed the Montessori approach would provide their daughter with the freedom she needed to be most successful.

Waldorf Method

The Waldorf method was developed by Rudolf Steiner in 1919 specifically for the children of employees who worked in the Waldorf-Astoria cigarette factory located in Germany.[10] The Waldorf program aims to develop children's strengths but also nurture areas in which they have challenges; ultimately the goal is to foster well-roundedness in each student. The Waldorf approach also aims to foster self-discipline among students. The Waldorf approach posits, "The best education is one that always expects children to be active thinkers and asks them to use their imaginations to produce assignments that show originality and effort and not just a recapitulation of facts."[11] Given the Waldorf approach's goal of fostering the whole child, standardized tests are not seen as effective measures of students' process because they encourage a narrow focus on facts and do not acknowledge children's creativity and other valuable traits. Instead, Waldorf teachers use a variety of assessment methods, including teacher observations and portfolios.

Portia, the veteran home educator of three sons, initially chose a charter school that followed the Waldorf method for her children's education. She explained her understanding of the Waldorf philosophy and what she liked about it for her sons:

> The principal of this charter school liked the Waldorf philosophy and started a charter school based on the Waldorf approach to teaching. After we got into the school, I read up on the Waldorf philosophy and the principles about why they did these things, and I thought this just makes so much sense. In kindergarten they cooked every week. Learning is not always just writing. Learning is developing their imaginations. Everyone is an artist. It is not that you are born with an art chromosome. If you develop the right side of the brain then you'll be creative, but most schools just want you to . . . once you enter kindergarten, your imagination is gone. Everything is about the left side, everything is cognitive. No more artsy stuff. So Waldorf's philosophy was to develop the left and right side of the brain at the same time. They did different things to develop both sides, and I thought, "This is so great!"

But when the principal's husband was relocated to another state by his employer, the principal left with him, and the Waldorf-based charter school was closed. Portia shared,

> That was rough on us because I loved their philosophy. They believe in music education. They learned the recorder in first grade. They learned German and again the art thing was really strong. They didn't believe in textbooks because they wanted the kids to develop their own imaginations. I just really, really loved that

> school for my sons. So after the school closed, then I put my kids in a public school. My sons at the time were fifth grade, third grade, and first grade. I put them in the public school for that one year and thought, "There goes four years of nurturing and art gone [*slams table*] down the drain in one year, because the art program was gone, and the music program was gone."

Continuing, she shared,

> They didn't have any music education for budget reasons; they threw it out thinking that it was not necessary. But to me music education is necessary. Then I saw the shift to clothing challenges. Waldorf never believed in uniforms because every child is unique. Their policy was you couldn't wear designer clothes like Sean John or Michael Jordan, so the kids just wore plain colored shirts and shoes. So no one was concerned if it was RocaWear or this or that. Well, we get to this school, and I hear, "Mommy I want a Sean John this or that." I'm thinking, you all have been in this school for, what, four or five months now and you are concerned about your clothes? In just that one year! I said, oh no, I'm not going to deal with this. I'm thinking about my first grader and I'm saying twelve more years of this? I don't think so!

Instructionally, the Waldorf charter school had a less stressful approach to test taking, even during the state-required standardized testing time. Portia shared,

> But I find now that a lot of public schools, not just [her state], a high percentage of them are just teaching the test. They are just teaching so that the kids can do decently on the test, and the state can say, they're meeting our expectations. Now, at my Waldorf charter school, my oldest son took the [state test]. The students didn't even know they were taking the [state] test. They just told us [parents] to make sure that your child has a nice breakfast, we will be doing the [state test] for one week. That was it. It was no big push! They [the school] got the Apple Award for the scores on those [state] tests for three years in a row. They did not stress. They did not try to teach just for that test, and the kids excelled on the test!

Portia found a school with a clearly defined educational philosophy that permeated all aspects of teaching and learning, and ideas that she supported wholeheartedly. The tenets of the Waldorf approach aligned with her ideas of what would work best for her sons. But when the school closed, she had to turn to home education to provide her sons with an education that would nurture their cognitive and creative abilities because her locally assigned public school was not able to meet that need. As noted earlier, Portia adapted the Charlotte Mason approach for her home education practice, which she found to be similar to the Waldorf approach.

John Holt: Unschooling

John Holt was an American educator who wrote numerous books, including *How Children Fail* (1964) and *How Children Learn* (1967), in which he puts forth the argument, like Charlotte Mason, that children have a built-in sense of curiosity that lends itself to learning on their own.[12] He suggested that, rather than enforcing a prescribed curriculum, educators should strive to learn the "ways, conditions, and spirit in which children do their best learning" and then create school environments that align with those ideals.[13] Holt believed it would be best for educators to allow students to direct their learning by encouraging them to ask for help when they need it, and trust children to learn in the proper environment. Educators would do best to provide inspiration and support for learning. Ultimately, Holt criticized public schools for their testing, rigid curriculum, and ability-grouping practices.[14] Holt's ideas undergird the unschooling movement, which embraces "learning and teaching that does not resemble school learning and teaching" and instead gives students as much freedom to direct their own learning as adults can tolerate.[15] Yolanda and her son in the second vignette that opened this chapter provided an example of unschooling. Not being from the South, her son wondered why the grass turned a beige color in the fall. This question turned into an entire lesson on not only the types of grasses but also the life cycle of plants and, more importantly, how to learn.

Blended Philosophies

In 2008, I conducted a focus group with close to twenty Black home educators, with the aim of better understanding their motivations and practices. When I asked parents to label their practice as traditional, unschooling, or other, all but one mother claimed their practice was "blended," meaning a little of both traditional and unschooling. Yet, interview after interview, Black home educators described their homeschool practice as having characteristics found across each of the four philosophies. Putting their children front and center in their learning meant engaging in a *child-centered* practice based in part on their *children's natural interests*. Black parents described curating learning experiences at home and within their communities that provided their children with *hands-on learning* opportunities. Black home educators created *portfolios* to document their children's learning even if they lived in states that did not require this. In addition, Black parents expressed that they strove to develop their *children's independence* in their learning and that they wanted their children to *love the process of learning* in and of itself so that they would be lifelong learners.

Overall, the educational philosophies of Mason, Montessori, and Holt and the Waldorf approach overlap with the twentieth century's Progressive Era of education. Teacher education students might not necessarily be introduced to Mason's or Holt's educational approaches, but they would likely be taught constructivism as developed by Progressive Era thinkers John Dewey and Lev Vygotsky. Each of these educational approaches and philosophies has distinctions, but they share a common bond in that they advocate that children should play an active role in their learning rather than remaining passive. In the next section, data from Black homeschool research will be presented to demonstrate the ways Black children have been able to transform in homeschool practices that put children first.

BLACK HOME EDUCATORS' FOLK PEDAGOGY IN PRACTICE

To fully understand and appreciate the transformative nature of Black home educators' children-first pedagogy, one must have clarity regarding the context surrounding their situation, including descriptions of the learner before homeschooling and then after implementation of Black home educators' pedagogy. Therefore, large extracts of direct quotes from one Black home educator have been provided in this section as an exemplar. Keep in mind, however, that no two families will have the same folk pedagogy. Our pedagogy regarding teaching, and how the brain works, will differ as a result of our experiences, our beliefs, and the children we are teaching.

Jessica is a single mother and home educator for her son and daughter. She is also an educational leader in her urban community. She is politically aware and has spent significant time reflecting on the lessons learned from her dual role as a mother and home educator. Jessica began homeschooling her son during his preK and kindergarten years. Due to health challenges during pregnancy with her daughter, she had to enroll her son in a private Christian school midway through kindergarten. In the middle of first grade, Jessica's health improved, and she pulled her son out of school to homeschool again. But then her daughter became ill, and her son had to return to school again. He had continued in public schools up until the year before our interview. He was currently in high school. Conversely, Jessica had homeschooled her daughter since she was in third grade, for health and special needs reasons. For this pedagogical example, I focus on Jessica's account of her most recent experience transitioning her son from public school back into homeschooling.

Jessica's pedagogy remains focused on putting her children's needs and interests first. For high school, Jessica chose to enroll her son in a "high-performing charter school high school." She explained her limited school choice options:

> I think this is probably happening across the country, but again, I can only speak to [my city], is charter schools moving into our neighborhoods and basically overtaking our traditional schools. We don't have any traditional high schools left anymore in this [neighborhood] and they come in promising really high academic outcomes and high graduation rates and all of that. But my son was in one of these charter schools for middle school, and they do every year, they have 100 percent college acceptance. So, no matter what, you have to apply for college through their program, and everybody gets accepted, even if it's a community college.

While attractive and admirable, the school's performance expectations of 100 percent college acceptance would place a lot of pressure on teachers and, Jessica soon discovered, on students as well. Jessica shared,

> But what we found is that really it becomes these spaces to control, I believe, Black and Brown bodies in a very prisonlike structure. And that's what my son had a really hard time with. So, you can't talk in the hallway, like a thousand rules around the smallest little things. So even having your coat on you, even in the winter, your coat must be in the locker. And if it's not, then you're going to get what they call, it's basically the equivalent of detention. They call it a refocus. And my son, who is already a very strong, A-type personality and loves to follow the rules, was having issues. He began to have so much anxiety around following the rules within the school building, but then also following the rules that were specific to assignments. So, you know, if the teacher said, do the math problem this way, if I showed him the old-school way, then it was just a problem. But it was a high-anxiety problem. Oh, too much. You know what I mean? So he would wake up at times at three and four o'clock in the morning, and we're talking middle school, sixth grade, "I must make sure my homework is okay. I must make sure my lunch is made. I must make sure that I'm on time for school." And then when he would come home from school, he would have complete meltdowns. I'm talking not even five minutes walking in the door, he's just screaming, crying, falling on the ground, totally distraught. And I would talk to his

> teachers and say, are you seeing this behavior? Like, something is going on, what is happening at school? They'd say, "He's great. He's an amazing kid." So whatever it was that he was dealing with, he'd be holding on to it until he got home, probably because he knew that it [home] was a safe space [to release it].

Jessica realized she had to go into the school to see what was happening there for herself. Recounting her observations, she stated,

> As I started showing up at the school more and more, I realized that this place was being run like a prison. And I don't think that when I looked at other charter schools that are moving into more affluent neighborhoods . . . the energy was totally different. The level of resources! Last year we did an equity bus tour where we went around to different schools within the [city area] to compare what was happening in these more affluent neighborhoods, like I'm saying, and ones that serve more underrepresented groups. I mean, from the hallways, how they're decorated, to access to clean water, even the privileges that the kids get, just night and day compared to what he experienced in his school. And when we're talking about race, I see that pattern where it's just trying to control Black and Brown bodies and then boasting about the outcomes, the academic outcomes as a result. But then we don't talk about the emotional trauma that's then happening. And that's really why I ended up homeschooling him this year and just pulling him out because he was so distressed, and it was ridiculous. You're too young to have this much stress and anxiety. Plus, he was at a high school where there was lots of police presence, and there was gang activity. They were constantly on lockdown or lockout or whatever the term is, where the kids can't leave the building, and he would call me when that was happening and just say, "Mom, I just don't want to be here. I just don't want to be here anymore." So yeah, that's why I think all of that has to do with race, but some of it just seems not overt. So more of a covert, right? Under-the-radar-type things, not the in-your-face racism.

Jessica shared her thoughts about how she approached homeschooling her son, especially given what he had experienced in school:

> This is my personal belief. So, for me, if I am perpetuating traditional models of thinking in my home, then I feel like I'm retraumatizing my children because basically I'm taking that public school model or even a private school model that was oppressing them and bringing it into the home. And I learned that early on with my daughter, that I didn't recognize that that's what I was doing. But you don't know, at least for me, I didn't know how to homeschool, so I just said, well, I'll do what the school is doing. And over time, I realized that that caused more problems.

Understandably, application of the same learning techniques would not be appropriate for her son. Rather than seeking a learning approach that sought to control students, Jessica leaned into implementing self-directed learning, which would seem to be the opposite of learning within the school. Recounting the underlying beliefs that informed her pedagogical decision-making, Jessica shared,

> The other thing that I firmly believe in and has worked miracles, honestly, in our homeschooling environment is self-directed learning. So the first semester with my son, I just took the time to assess where he was emotionally and where he was academically just by observing and just saying, well, "What is it that you want to do?" "What is it that you want to learn?" And just kind of went on that journey with him. He automatically went into that normal public school stress mode. But I allowed that to happen so that we could have a conversation around why is this, what is this about? I have dialectical behavior therapy [DBT] cards and mindfulness cards that help him process when something is coming up for him. So we could start digging deep into what's what, and asking, "What are you believing about yourself that is leading you to this anxious behavior?" DBT is a form of mindfulness. So it helps him recognize his behavior. And the other one is cognitive behavioral therapy too, so that you have this rationalization around your emotions basically in a framework on how to deal with it. And then for us, we're also a Christian family, so we spend a lot of time praying and our faith, what does the Bible say about these things? And how can you be encouraged through that? What does God say about who you are and what he's expecting of you? And really, he just wants you to be the creation, the awesome creation that you already are, you know?

After summarizing her approach to home education for that first year, Jessica began to describe the transformation she observed in her son. She shared,

> I used that first semester to do that, where we did not have any expectations for performance. And once he had that space, and we worked through a lot of that drama, this second semester has been mind-blowing, probably more than I could have ever imagined. So his writing was atrocious, like last year, I said, "Are they teaching you how to write in English class? What are you actually doing?" I would read his papers and I didn't understand. So that was one of my big things when I brought him home, I said, "We're going to work on writing." We tried a traditional writing program, and it wasn't working for him. So when we went on the equity bus tour, I brought my kids, they were the only kids on it, but that started sparking a conversation around social justice and education. And he decided he wanted to write a paper. And so out of that, that's how we workshopped how to write a five-paragraph essay.

The equity bus tour gave her son something that he wanted to write about, and Jessica continued to explain how the spark grew into a flame. She stated,

> It was out of something that he was interested in versus me putting a curriculum in front of him. So that's one thing. And then let me tell you, from that paper to his second paper, which was an article in a local journal that asked him to be a student voice. To see night and day, just from workshopping that one paper for him, this second paper. . . . Man! And then it was good enough to publish! So then the next step from that was working on a grant for his podcast. He wants to do a podcast! So he wrote a grant and got $2,000, and I've helped him with that. The second grant he just got, he asked for $10,000. This kid is bold. He wrote this grant totally on his own this time! Again, just like these amazing leaps!

Jessica's intuition led her to include her children on the equity bus tour, but she had no idea what that experience would do for her son as a learner. Not only did it give him something to write about, but it also led him to want to share with others in a very public way through a podcast. The equity bus trip enabled him to see the school-to-school inequities within his community, which in turn created a passion for the topic of social justice inequities.

Reflecting on how her son's transformation affected her, Jessica shared,

> I mean, it's my kid and I'm boasting on him. But really, I'm so passionate about homeschooling now because I want other families to hear these stories and see the freedom in it. And there's so much more potential there than I think a lot of times the public school is expecting from our children. Their low expectations cause them to not even get a chance to explore and shoot for the . . . I tell my kids, shoot for the stars, and you just might land on the moon. But if your teachers do not have high expectations, you never even try. And you don't have an adult in educational spaces that gives you permission to be creative and think outside of the box. So pulling them out of school was the first step, but then it's also for us to allow space for complete self-directed learning. I still believe in Mom having wisdom and having lived long enough to say, well, if you go down that road it might not be so great for you. So maybe let's just kind of bring it back in. But that's a balance of me as an elder, giving wisdom, but the level of, even with just within the emotional healing for my son in one semester is total night and day, even with making mistakes. So now he might make a mistake, and then it's more of a conversation around what he learned. And I modeled that for him, and now I see him doing it on his own, and he's more willing to not be right all the time. So yeah, I love that. And I think a lot of it is really changing our mind-set from being dictators of our children's education.

Jessica's home education pedagogy opened the world for her son by giving him a sense of purpose and meaning for his writing. However, she did not plan to do this. As she stated, she did not dictate her children's education. Instead, she used her instincts, focused on her son's needs, and trusted the process by giving her son the space he needed to find his way. The beliefs undergirding her pedagogical practice included a blend of her faith, strategies learned through mental health experiences, and her instincts related to determining what her son needed.

When Jessica realized how anxious her son's charter school environment had made him, she knew she needed to create a learning space that represented the opposite of that school setting. Recall that Jessica had described her son's charter school as "spaces to control" and "prisonlike," which she believed led to his anxiety. To begin to undo this, she engaged in a process of "deschooling," which is sometimes the first step unschoolers take to help transition students from traditional school.[16] Whereas students in traditional schools usually follow a set curriculum, routine, and schedule—or as Jessica sees it, have their education dictated to them—unschoolers serve as the authors and architects of their educational experiences. However, students who are transitioning from traditional schools often must unlearn the expectation of being told what to do, when to do it, and how to do it as a way of learning. This takes time.

While in the deschooling space, Jessica used the dialectical behavior therapy she had learned from another experience to help her son decompress and reframe his thinking around what learning could be for him. She asked reflective questions intended to get her son to reconsider why he thought what he thought about learning, which eventually enabled him to consider what he wanted to learn and how he wanted to learn. She also integrated their family's Christian faith into her deschooling process for additional grounding and guidance in the reframing process.

Instinctively, Jessica took her children on the equity bus tour of their city, and this had an unexpected result. Witnessing the limited resources in some schools compared with others in their city had a profound impact on her son. As parents and teachers, we never know how our children and youth will respond to experiences, but they do respond and that is the point. John Dewey's concept of experiential learning explicitly informs us that students learn best through experiences.[17] It is up to us to facilitate and curate those learning experiences and opportunities and to trust the process will be educational for our children, but as Jessica shared, developing this type of trust in yourself as an educator and in your children does not automatically happen and it takes time to develop.

BLACK HOME EDUCATORS' FOLK PEDAGOGY: IMPLICATIONS FOR ANYONE AND ANYWHERE

Each Black home educator's pedagogical approach represents a unique set of influences, including their beliefs, their experiences, and the needs of their children. How can such an idiosyncratic process inform teaching and learning approaches that put children first in other settings?

First, Jessica's example demonstrates the significance of self-reflection in the development of our teacher practice. In reflecting on her educator practice, Jessica carefully considered the impact of her instruction on her children. But she did not just assess her children's learning; she also observed how they were showing up as learners in the educational setting she had created for them. If we believe students should enjoy learning, then we need to monitor whether this is happening within our educational settings, even with a curriculum that has been prescribed to us as educators. In those settings with prescribed curriculums, educators will need to be creative to infuse the joy of learning in their students.

When I taught second grade, my public magnet school adhered to the Dewey-inspired Bank Street curriculum. For us, being Bank Steet inspired and required us to employ a child-centered approach to instruction and to place social studies at the forefront of our curriculum. We taught thematic units across the grade levels. In second grade we taught units such as Our City and Community Helpers. In this unit, students visited places in our city such as a hospital, the post office, and a restaurant to learn about the different roles, simple machines, and responsibilities needed in those settings.

One of the culminating projects for the unit required each second-grade class to transform into a functioning restaurant with a theme of their choosing. My themes always stemmed from my observations of students' interests over the school year. For example, observing the books my students took out from our media center week after week, I noticed their fascination with David Macaulay's book *The Way Things Work*. One day, they became completely enthralled with castles when they discovered the simple machines used in their defense mechanisms like pulleys and levers. Other students were into princesses and princes, horses, and the moats that encircled castles. So to prepare for a castle-themed restaurant, we studied the Middle Ages in comparison to what we had learned about life in our city, past and present. As they learned details of the Middle Ages and castle life, they incorporated that knowledge into our restaurant. Our menu had a slightly spicy shake-and-bake chicken dish that the students called Murder Hole Chicken. The murder hole was a part of the castle's defensive mechanism from which fire would rain down on enemies as they tried to cross the moat to attack the castle. The restaurants in my classroom became a celebration of my students' interests and yearlong learning beyond the curriculum. My child-centered restaurants meant that every year there was a new theme; some of the other themes were Italian food and the Rainforest Café.

Asking ourselves how our students are receiving our instruction is critical for our day-to-day instruction, not just special projects. In second grade, students had to learn how to tell time on an analog clock. To make this fun, I purchased ink stamps with blank analog clocks because many of my students enjoyed "playing school" in the learning center areas. I thought they would enjoy creating worksheets for each other to practice telling time. But I quickly realized the students did not fully comprehend analog time telling. On the spur of the moment, I called everyone to the carpet area and had twelve students stand in a circle, each representing a number on a clock. Then I had a student stand in the middle with the class broom (minute hand) and our yardstick (hour hand). We made note of the oddity of the fact that the longer hand (broom) represented the shorter unit of time (minute). Then I asked the person in the middle to show us various times for the hour, half hour, and quarter hour. More than anything else I would have planned, this activity of becoming a clock helped them understand telling time. It was not in my lesson plans. It was a spur-of-the-moment decision based on what I observed in my students. Sometimes these unplanned shifts in our instruction are our best lessons. Yet, in some educational settings, teachers do not have the professional freedom to make such spur-of-the-moment decisions.

How do educational professionals, administrators, and policy makers create spaces for teacher self-reflection as a valid form of professional development? Where is there space in teacher education programs for emerging teachers to engage in self-reflection to identify the influences on their folk pedagogy before they enter their own classrooms? What we think about our thinking on our teaching (our metacognition) is an important part of understanding our folk pedagogy as educators. Typically, teachers' professional development opportunities are limited to learning a new curriculum program or best practices. However, these types of professional development do not have our specific students and learning contexts in mind. Like Jessica and other Black home educators, teachers need space and time to explore their teacher metacognition. Creating space for teachers to examine their thinking about their teaching would be fruitful in fostering teachers' ability to meet students' needs and improve learning outcomes.[18]

A pedagogical stance of putting children first requires all educators to consider all aspects of our learners' beings. Emotional, psychological, and physical challenges can often become barriers to learning. Home educators have the flexibility and space to change their plans for the day to accommodate those challenges. Educators in traditional school settings frequently do not. Moreover, there is sometimes a culture that requires everyone to do the same thing in traditional settings. However, this type of school culture does not have to exist. For example, when I was a teacher in the 1990s, before No Child Left Behind, I had the flexibility to alter my daily schedule to align with my students' needs. I taught math in flexible mastery groups based on what students needed. This meant that on some days a student might meet with me in two different small groups for math, if they needed extra support. While I worked on math groups, my students often could choose to work on their writing workshop papers, read their books, work in one of our learning centers, or work on their social studies research projects. We always had something that was in process, and they had the freedom to choose how to use that time.

You may be wondering, given today's more restrictive teaching environment, how teachers today might implement child-first pedagogy. Here is a list of ideas representing small steps toward creating educational justice for the children in your classrooms:

- Morning meetings: Classrooms can have morning meetings, which are opportunities to set the tone and purpose for the day, build community, and review content knowledge.[19] To me, morning meeting spaces deploy the humanity of teaching and learning. Students can express how they are feeling and what is on their minds as school begins. This helps them transition from whatever they left at home and whatever may have happened on their journey to school. Morning meetings are spaces where students practice embracing differences and discover what they have in common with their classmates. These spaces can also become student led after we model each component of them. As such, morning meetings are a space for student voice and choice. Morning meetings are commonly associated with elementary classrooms, but they can be used in the middle grades.[20] I use a variation of morning meetings in my higher education courses, where evening classes have "evening meeting" to model the practice for pre- and in-service educators. Therefore, I believe morning meetings could be adapted to fit the needs of high school classrooms and homerooms as well. I also found it extremely valuable to have a brief afternoon meeting following lunch and recess, just to get the children focused again for the remainder of the day.

- Openings and closings of lessons: The lessons teachers teach should be structured with an opening, practice and development, and a closing. This is just good professional practice. But saying, "Open your books to page 99," does not fully take advantage of what the opening of a lesson could do for students. Instead, openings that invite our students to wonder, reflect, or even recall create opportunities to tap into our students' prior knowledge; to either build on what they have only just learned or to generate students' prior experiences or knowledge of a new topic. Our openings can spark student interest, if we take the time to consider ways to invite our students to engage in what they are about to learn. Examples include selecting an artifact of a particular historical era to be studied and asking students to figure out what it is and how it was used (e.g., a railroad tie to start a unit on the role of the railroad during the Civil War). Students rarely get up close to a railroad tie. You can find them at flea markets or even online. Similarly, closings can serve as opportunities for students to share their thoughts about what they have learned.

    Both openings and closings provide opportunities for students to connect and relate to what they are learning in personal ways, and this can be done in relatively limited amounts of time. Devoting these few moments to our students' thoughts and ideas puts them first and enables us to see where they are in their understanding of the content; openings and closings can serve as an authentic type of formative assessment for teachers.
- Student questions: One of the best ways to put students first in their education is to not ignore their questions and wonderings that emerge as

they learn. As educators today, time sometimes becomes our master. So much so that when our students ask a question that is not directly related to what we want them to learn, we will brush it off. District pacing guides and testing place this pressure on us. But consider that students' questions represent their connection to the content, even if they take you away from your objectives a bit. For example, while I was teaching fourth grade, required reading included the book *Mr. Popper's Penguins*. As the children read the book, they started asking, "Can penguins really open a refrigerator door?" "Do penguins really collect stuff to pile up like that?" "Do penguins . . . ?" Now, as their teacher, I did not know the answers to those questions, and nothing in the curriculum surrounding this fictional text suggested a study of penguins specifically. I had a choice: I could say, "I don't know," each time they asked and continue on the expected trajectory of the curriculum, or I could gather their questions and find a way for us to learn the answers. My classroom almost always had questions under investigation. The questions typically came from my students and only tangentially related to our district curriculum. These were my students' wonderings. I did not have the heart to ignore them. I would enlist the help of our media center specialist to find sources to answer their questions. We created graphic organizers that hung on our classroom walls to record the "data" as each student learned something new. This kept us from duplicating our efforts. I invited parents to help us with this exploration as well. At the time, we had just been given internet access in our classroom. The curriculum required us to teach the conventions of letter writing. I thought, An email is a type of letter, right? So we composed emails to penguin gurus (found by searching the internet) with the nomenclature associated with letter writing (salutation, introduction, body, etc.) and waited in excited anticipation for their responses.

Now, I do not remember how long the exploration into penguins lasted, but I can tell you that it did not take away from our curriculum-prescribed instruction, though my administrator at the time did raise some questions. The penguin study became part of our morning meeting routine through student reports, and the media center specialist used it to address her instructional needs. No direct instruction time used! To wrap up our study, I asked the students to compare the penguin facts we learned with the way

> penguins were portrayed in the book. Students completed this task as part of a learning center, while I taught subject areas in small groups. I used the results of this assignment to create a black-and-white bulletin board display in the hallway outside our classroom, which we titled "Mr. Popper's Penguins—Fact vs. Fiction." The bulletin board display led my principal to question the happenings in my classroom. I explained, and to be perfectly honest, he did not like it. But shortly after our conversation, the district asked him to send the names of teachers who had successfully integrated the internet in their instruction. Guess whose name he gave them? When an article favorably featuring our fourth-grade penguin study appeared in the local newspaper, my principal fully apologized and said he was grateful for my work honoring our students' sense of curiosity. Putting children first is honoring this sense of curiosity!

Overall, the folk pedagogy of Black home educators integrates elements of professional freedom that traditional teachers may appear to have limited access to today. But with teachers' creativity and courage, children can assume ownership of their education through voice and choice. To explore this notion from the perspective of educators, the next chapter presents educational justice from the perspective of former teachers who left teaching positions to assume the role of home educator to their children and sometimes for other people's children as well.

CHAPTER 4

Former Black Teachers Choosing Home Education

Tamara, a public school teacher with thirteen years of experience who was located in a rural community, shared why she resigned from teaching at her middle school midyear when she had just reached tenure. Two years before resigning from her teaching position, Tamara had begun homeschooling her sixth-grade son. She shared,

> As of this year, I had been teaching long enough to have seen almost every student from when I began teaching graduate from high school. So that would have been the first class. But, you know, when administrators start telling you what you are not doing in this virtual setting, when there's no blueprint for how to teach this type of child in a virtual setting, then it is time for me to go. I miss the interaction. I miss my colleagues because they had become my family; they became my friends. But do I miss people telling me what to do? What not to do? Telling me I'm not good enough, not giving me credit when credit is due? Hovering over me and being a helicopter when I've been doing this longer than some of them who are now in administration, and I have two degrees? I remember going to a training one time and they had just developed a new curriculum, and the person that was leading it was asking how much teaching experience each of us had. And at that point I had maybe eight years of experience, somebody else had fifteen, somebody else had about twenty. And we asked her, "How long have you been teaching?" She said, "Oh, this is my third year." Girl, bye! What can you tell me? You ain't even built up an immunity to the students yet. What are you talking about? Those people who are above us still treat us like we don't know what we are talking about as teachers. We're just looked at as, you know, novice students. We're not even viewed as novice teachers; we're treated like novice

> students. It feels like my degrees meant nothing. That's the type of stuff that would burn my biscuits.

The US is experiencing a nationwide teacher shortage. Approximately nine out of every ten school districts reported difficulties in hiring teachers in 2023.[1] At the start of the 2023–24 school year, 45 percent of public schools reported teaching shortages, which is a slight improvement over the previous year, when 50 percent of public schools were understaffed. Yet teacher vacancies outweigh the rate of new hires.[2] Moreover, high-poverty school communities had higher rates of understaffing compared with the national rate. Further, trends suggest that Black teachers plan to leave their classrooms at higher rates than teachers overall. To address the teacher shortage, the US Department of Education has established initiatives aimed at raising teacher salaries, supporting strong teacher induction programs, increasing teacher leadership opportunities, and collaborating with teacher preparation programs.[3]

However, as shown in Tamara's vignette, it is not a lack of leadership opportunities, teacher preparation practices, induction programs, or even salary issues that Black home educators identify as the reasons they leave their classrooms. Therefore, none of the national initiatives get to the heart of why twelve Black teachers in my research reported leaving their classrooms to homeschool their children and other people's children. Instead, former Black teachers are seeking educational justice through the respect and professional freedom they find in the home education community.

A lack of respect for teachers' experience and knowledge has contributed to the teacher shortage and declining enrollment in teacher education programs. In 2010 Diane Ravitch—an education historian who had supported the No Child Left Behind Act ten years earlier—reversed her beliefs regarding the role of testing and of ramped-up accountability in education.[4] In a complete turnaround, in her newer publications she demonstrated how No Child Left Behind and all its components have undermined the teaching profession. She explained that aligning the evaluation of teachers to test scores had oversimplified the definition of effective teaching. She argued that teachers should be evaluated by master teachers and peer review rather than by relying on test scores.[5] Tamara's opening vignette provides a peek into the challenging climate many teachers work in today. However, these are not the only factors that influence Black teachers' decisions to become home educators. In this chapter, I address the questions, What motivates Black teachers to become home educators, and what forms of educational justice do they create as a result?

This book conceptualizes educational justice through the lens of Black home education as child privacy protection, where students have the freedom "to be and become."[6] For teachers, privacy protection aligns with the notion of professional freedom. Teaching is a profession, and therefore teachers need professional freedom to do their jobs effectively. In a recent op-ed, a superintendent emphasized the importance of educators' professional freedom when building an engaged teacher workforce: "The key to fostering a positive environment for teaching and learning has remained the same before, during, and after the pandemic. We believe our teachers are committed and capable educators and we give them the freedom to prove it."[7] *Professional freedom* refers to respecting the professionalism of educators from preschool through high school in the same way the professional freedom of lawyers and doctors is respected. It requires giving teachers the space to make pedagogical decisions to meet their students' needs without scripts and other impingements on their professional decision-making.

This chapter explores Black teachers' decisions to homeschool as they relate to the protection of their children's privacy as mothers and the protection of their professional practice as educators. In addition, former Black teachers share the emotional challenges and labor of advocating for their children, sometimes even when they taught in the same school their children attended. The chapter ends with suggestions to guard teacher professionalism in preK through twelfth-grade education.

OVERVIEW OF FOCAL BLACK TEACHERS

The eight Black home educators featured in this chapter include classroom teachers, a media specialist, and a daycare teacher. These educator moms had taught from one year to over twenty years. Most (five) participating former educators had eight or more years of teaching experience. Three former teachers were in their first three years of homeschooling at the time of the study. As indicated in table 4.1, Black home educators transitioned from their classrooms to home education in different ways. Alayah, Amber, Kate, and Tamara left their public school classrooms to homeschool their children. Alayah homeschooled other people's children as well as her own, and Tamara served as a homeschool consultant and tutor.

TABLE 4.1 Demographic overview of Black teachers who became home educators

Former educator	*Type of school and number of years*	*Years in home education*	*Transition to homeschooling*
Alayah	Urban public elementary, 6 years	3 years	Left her classroom when her son was born. Homeschooled her son from birth and started a business homeschooling other people's children.
Amber	Rural public elementary, 20+ years	20+ years	Pulled her children in and out of schools to homeschool them as she maintained her teaching career. She started a private school/program in the community.
Charlise	Urban public elementary, 7 years Urban elementary, 2 years Urban elementary, 2 Years	20+ years	Taught special needs in elementary school before becoming a home educator. She pulled her oldest child out of a private second grade to homeschool.
Hope	Adult education and preschool teacher (special education), 7 years	8 years	Taught preschool while her oldest was also in preschool. Then she began homeschooling. While her husband was overseas in the military, she placed both children in a private Christian school while she went back to school for teacher certification. Then she went back to homeschooling.
Kate	Urban public middle school, 7 years	1 year	Taught English for Speakers of Other Languages in middle grades and also taught in higher education. Always wanted to homeschool. Children turned school age (four and five) and she left teaching to home educate them.
Tamara	Rural middle school, 13 years	2 tears	Started homeschooling her son in the sixth grade while teaching full time. Left her classroom two years later after thirteen years of teaching.
Tempest	Urban private Catholic elementary (media specialist), 1 year	8 years	Homeschooled her sister before homeschooling her own children. Taught technology and served as the librarian/media center specialist in the private Christian school her children attended. Removed her children from the school to homeschool them.
Venera	Urban private daycare provider	14 years	Served as a daycare provider for 2 years in her community while also homeschooling her children.

Amber homeschooled while teaching in public schools until she eventually opened a private school of her own. Charlise, Hope, Tempest, and Venera removed their children from private Christian schools to homeschool. Tempest left a private Christian school where she had served as a teacher to homeschool.

Though these Black teacher-mothers transitioned to home education differently, their insider knowledge as educators and motherly understanding of their children greatly informed the decision to homeschool. Next, I will further explore factors that informed these mothers' decisions to homeschool.

BLACK TEACHERS' MOTIVATIONS FOR BECOMING HOME EDUCATORS

This section focuses on the decision-making motivations of teacher-mothers who taught in classrooms before deciding to homeschool their children. Tamara was the only single parent in the group; the remaining mothers were married when they initially chose to homeschool. Married teacher-mothers made decisions in consultation with their husbands. Three factors that influenced Black teachers' decisions to become home educators were differences between their dreams and reality, the inflexibility of traditional school settings (public and private), and a mismatch between their children's personalities and needs, on one hand, and the school's structure, on the other.

Dreams Differed from Reality

Many mothers who left their classrooms to homeschool originally dreamed of becoming stay-at-home mothers when they had children or imagined that their children would attend "good schools." But those dreams differed from the reality they experienced. The dreams Alayah talked about with her husband even varied from her private imagination. She explained, "When my husband and I first got married, we talked about kids and always planned that I would be home. But then, in my head, I still pictured that since I'm a schoolteacher, when it's time for him [her oldest child] to go back to school, he would just come to the school I taught in. He would be right there with me. You know, I would be able to keep watch over what he's learning and stuff like that." So even though Alayah planned to stay home with her children, she imagined returning to her classroom with her children at some point. Instead, she continued to homeschool her children after they reached school age. Conversely, Tempest had the situation Alayah dreamed of; she was teaching in the private Catholic school her children attended. She, however, would ultimately leave her teaching position to homeschool her children.

Unlike Alayah and Tempest, Hope dreamed of being a career-minded mother. She shared, "When I went to college, I wanted to become a physician, but I kept fainting in the emergency room. So I went into public health instead. And so, after graduating with my bachelor's in public health, I started working in a welfare-to-work program. I was teaching anatomy and physiology classes to women interested in health careers." The women frequently had to bring their children to class, and Hope explained, "They were little, like in kindergarten, so I taught them during our break, trying to find activities just to keep them active or entertained. I enjoyed that more, so from there I started working part time at a preschool." When Hope had her first child, she left her preschool classroom to homeschool, even though homeschooling was not part of her plan. She shared, "I didn't plan it [homeschooling] because I thought, okay, I'm going to get my certification, I'm going to teach. I love school." Like many home educators, Hope gave up her career goals to homeschool her children.

Kate, an adjunct educator, placed her children in daycare when she had a teaching assignment at a local university but kept them home with her when she was not teaching. She explained, "This is the first year that I've just declared it as homeschooling, but I've had them at home since birth except for here and there [when she was teaching]. I'm a teacher and I teach occasionally at [a local university], so I go back and forth. Sometimes I'd have them in preschool, but then this past year, I officially declared it as homeschooling." She described her decision as follows: "Really it just was a mental—kind of like a paradigm shift because I would be called [by the university] so much for teaching jobs, so it was really very easy not to have a definite decision in mind [with regard to her children's education]. But this time, I really had to declare that we were homeschooling because my oldest was five." State law required five-year-old children to attend public school, so the law forced Kate to make a definitive decision.

Tamara also left teaching to homeschool her son, but she spent two years homeschooling him while also teaching at her school before deciding to homeschool him full time. As described in the opening vignette of this chapter, Tamara's administration and school setting led her to leave her classroom mid–school year. Homeschooling was not a part of her initial dream for her son.

Like many of the other homeschoolers, Charlise and her husband did not initially have home education in mind for their children. She explained,

> Before having children, we discussed what our children's education would look like. However, being where we came from, quite frankly, what we both had envisioned was that we would raise our kids a certain way, and we saw ourselves as climbing that ladder, moving out of coming from families who were working lower-income people to moving up to being middle income. At that point, we were young. We said, "Oh, our kids would definitely go to good schools." And what good schools meant to us, we didn't necessarily think private. But we thought if you move to a very good area, you send your kid to a good school, and so that's what starts you off. That's what I thought, and that's what we both thought.

They moved outside the large urban district where Charlise taught, but she and her husband soon realized that the schools there, while considered by many to be quite good, did not live up to their expectations. "When we had children, we even moved to [a suburban school district], which was supposed to be one of the best school districts. As a matter of fact, our school was even named a [state school of excellence], but we quickly found out that wasn't what we thought it should be," Charlise explained. "What the public schools called excellence wasn't necessarily what we equated with excellence. We didn't want our kids to be statistics, particularly my son, as a Black male. We didn't want him to be a statistic." As an educator, Charlise had hoped to find a focus on mastery of skills and content rather than learning through memorization. Charlise and her husband decided to place their oldest child in a private Christian school, which will be discussed in the next section.

Overall, these former teachers did not intend to homeschool their children, even if they planned to be stay-at-home mothers. Deciding to homeschool meant leaving behind careers that they had invested years of preparation to obtain. They sometimes oscillated between their careers, preschool, and homeschooling before fully committing to full-time home education. The next section describes how the inflexible nature of school settings, both public and private, contributed to these Black teachers' homeschool decisions.

The Rigidity of Traditional Schools (Public and Private)

As educators, former teachers who left their classrooms to homeschool their children hold insider knowledge regarding the inner workings of schools. This section demonstrates how teacher-mothers' knowledge of school contexts from their insider perspective informed their home education decisions.

The rigidity of school settings, whether public or private, emerged as a factor in teachers' decision to turn to home education as they described beliefs regarding the learning process, their children's personalities and abilities, and the purpose of learning. For example, Kate's motivation to homeschool emerged before she had children of her own. Reflecting on her beliefs regarding the process of learning, she explained,

> It really resonated with me early—even before I had children, I knew I wanted to homeschool. One, because I'm a teacher and I love the learning process and I just think that it's not very respected in school, which is ironic. But I think that things like critical thinking, the love of learning, exploration, and investigation should be in the school. But children very early on get subtle messages these things are not the point of the whole "schooling thing" and that it's more about following rules. I don't even mean this in a bad way. I'm not a school basher. I think that schools have amazing potential. I think that teachers are the best people in the world, and they really adore their classrooms when the teacher is there for children. I just think that the root of the problem is the system of school. And so, making all those observations before I had kids. . . . Especially in public school, you see so many of them falling through the cracks who are very intelligent in other areas but maybe not in the traditional areas or normal ways. I just know I didn't want to put my kids through that.

Kate's insider knowledge led her to believe that public school norms overlooked students who did not demonstrate their abilities in "normal ways." Her observations suggested that some children unknowingly experience a lack of sociocultural synchronization between home and school.[8] This means that children whose home context did not align with school expectations did not fare as well as children whose home lives mirrored school expectations. Typically, low-income, Black, and Brown children experience such a lack of sociocultural synchronization.[9] Because of this, teachers and other school staff may view such students from a deficit perspective or ignore or not recognize their potential. Kate believed she had observed this phenomenon in her school as a teacher, which led her to think school norms focused more on following rules rather than on instilling a love of learning in the students and developing their critical thinking skills.

Similarly, Charlise, a former public school teacher, initially placed her son in a private Christian school after determining that the public school she taught in did not measure up to her standards of excellence. Charlise and her husband turned to homeschooling when their son entered third grade because the school taught everything through memorization (as she had found in the public school), and as a result, her son was not learning. She explained, "Usually most of us, hopefully when we taught our kids math, we gave them three blocks or three objects and then said three plus three, now count them. They're six. So they begin to visualize as well as experience things concretely. But a lot of times in this school, that's not what they were doing. Instead, they were doing it by rote. So we didn't like that school. He was scoring high on the standardized tests, so that was never an issue, but he wasn't learning for growth." The focus on rote learning, or memorization, meant that her son did not have the conceptual understanding that she expected as an educator. Learning by memorization conflicts with educational theories such as constructivism, which tells us that students learn best when they can actively engage with content or skills. This suggests that having students apply what they have learned is a more effective approach to teaching than using passive rote teaching methods.[10]

Alayah, a former first-grade public school teacher, homeschooled her son from birth and then decided not to go back to her classroom. When her son got old enough to go to school, she remembered, "Thinking of my old coworkers who . . . a lot of people get into teaching because you get the summers off—so thinking of how it's almost one of those things where it's a roll of the dice. There are good teachers in the public school system but it's a roll of the dice, to me . . . whether you get that good teacher." Alayah's teaching experience led her to question some of her colleagues' commitment to teaching and their teaching effectiveness. From her perspective, she had no guarantee that her son would always have the best teacher, even if she taught in the same school her child attended. This indicates that Alayah did not trust that her insider role as a teacher would offer any advantage in her son's educational experience.

Black home educators who were former educators themselves also found private school contexts unacceptable for their children's learning needs. Venera, a public school teacher, moved from one state to another. Preconceived ideas about the public schools in her new state weighed heavily in her decision to place her oldest child, a son, in a private school. She shared,

> I relocated from [a northern state] and I moved to [a southern state] just to get away from the cold weather. But I knew the schools weren't comparable to [the northern state's], so I always had a plan that if I didn't like what I saw,

> then I would put them in private school. So that's basically what happened. My oldest ended up in private school and did fine. Unfortunately, a lot of Christian private schools combine classes when their enrollment decreases. They combine grades. And so he struggled and struggled, and it got to the point the last year that I just brought him home. At that time, I had met people who were homeschooling their children at church. So I just started working with him at home and he seemed to do much better. The next year I just kept him home—that was fifth grade—and worked with him from fifth grade up to tenth grade. Then we had family problems. I was separated, so I put him back in school for high school. He did a little bit of tenth grade and then he did eleventh and twelfth grade. But I could see his work was just going downhill and he didn't do really well.

Venera's account demonstrates that Christian private schools do not always address all students' learning needs. Limited resources most likely led to the need to create mixed-grade classes, which did not serve her son well. She shared, "I started homeschooling because I cared about him learning. I wanted to make sure he could read and that he could do basic functions, a lot of mental math, and just be, to me, a very literate person and to be able to get a good job. And so, I felt like it was my responsibility as his mother—I'm the first teacher he had, I taught him how to sit at the table, I taught him how to not run across the street, and how to get dressed. And so, therefore, I could teach him the things he needed." Reminiscent of the experiences of other home educators found in the literature, Venera's beliefs about motherhood informed her decision to homeschool.[11] But being a professional educator also influenced her decision to homeschool.

Interestingly, Venera chose not to get licensed to teach in her new state. She explained, "I was a teacher. I just didn't have my license in [the new state]. I had gone to college. I finished. I got a bachelor's in [the former state]. But nobody knew that. I never—because the thing whenever we have our support group meetings, I never wanted that to be an issue—'Well, you can do it because you have a . . .'—nobody ever knew it." Venera believed that by keeping her teaching credentials private, she could best remain on equal footing with the other homeschool moms in the support groups. She did not want to seem like an "expert." Home educating your own child differs a great deal from teaching a classroom of children in a school because home educators carry the emotional burden of motherhood.

Reflecting on her home education decision, Venera further shared,

> When I finally went back to work as a teacher, they were like, "You were a teacher all along?" Like, yeah. And they were just shocked, you know, "You didn't act like one." I was like, okay, "What does that mean? Am I supposed to act like one?" But because people would say, you know, sometimes people would say, well, "You must have a certificate to teach your children." I'm like, "No, you don't." Who loves them more? I mean, the greatest thing that really convinced me, my son was struggling, and he had to go to school with thirty strangers and spend more time with the thirty strangers than with me. And I was like, something's wrong with this picture. I need to put that devotion and loyalty to my son and my daughter first.

Venera's transition from classroom teacher to home educator began with a negative perception of the public schools in the new state she lived in, which led her to a private school. But when conditions in the private school did not support her son's learning needs, Venera-the-mother and Venera-the-teacher bonded to step in and assume full responsibility for his education.

Similarly, Tempest, a former media center specialist in a private Christian school, initially homeschooled her younger sister, who was in sixth grade, and then turned to homeschooling both of her own children as well. She shared, "I was desperate to help my little sister succeed in school. She was a brilliant child who was beaten down by the system because she didn't learn the way traditional schools teach." Before homeschooling, Tempest's sister and children attended the private Christian school where Tempest worked. Her insider knowledge included observations of how other students were treated. For example, she shared, "So I'm watching, and some kids come in with problems. They were diagnosed as ADD [attention deficit disorder], ADHD [attention deficit hyperactivity disorder], or having some other issue. And most of these kids who were diagnosed this way are African American. For the most part, the teachers did not want to deal with kids who had any kind of issue at all. They thought that, 'We're not trained to do this. We're not equipped to do this; we shouldn't have to do this.' And those that needed that special attention just didn't get it." The literature on Black students and special education, and on ADD/ADHD in particular, is not always conclusive. Medical research has found that Black students have a higher rate of ADD/ADHD diagnosis than the overall public.[12] Yet, other recent research suggests there is a high rate of underdiagnosis among Black students when compared with White students. The stigma surrounding ADHD may contribute to the underdiagnosis of Black children.[13] Race and social class appear to be associated with issues in diagnosing ADHD, whether overdiagnosed or underdiagnosed.[14] Reports have documented problematic implementation of special education programs, revealing that they have been used to intentionally get Black children who have been deemed troublesome due to their behavior out of general education classrooms.[15]

Like Charlise, Tempest also observed a focus on tests rather than in-depth learning. She explained,

> I know the state has standards, but in my state, here's what I found: kids in school can answer a question quickly. They're quick to want to be the first one to try to answer the question; they're not always so accurate with their answers. But it is okay to just have an answer. I also found that when we asked them questions, just about . . . anything, about a science question like, "Do you recognize this, do you know what this is?" in a conversation, they're not able to respond. A lot of them know how to take tests, but they don't know how to take that knowledge and be able to integrate it into everyday life, with conversations, just you know, putting things together.

As an educator, Tempest, like other homeschool mothers, desired to see children using their critical thinking skills to make connections. However, it is challenging to make those connections if you are taught content in isolation or through rote memorization without opportunities to apply what you learn to real-life situations. Such opportunities were often absent because educators were not given the professional freedom to create them in their schools.

Attempting to support her younger sister, Tempest enrolled her in the private Christian school she worked in and her children attended. However, transferring to the new school setting was challenging for her sister; the other students did not readily accept her. When Tempest told the administrators about her sister's challenge in being accepted, they responded, "Well, these students have been together since they were three years old"—meaning they had formed strong bonds. Tempest responded, "Yeah, but when do you teach them that they have to welcome other people in?" Tempest continued, "So I took it upon myself in the library to start doing something about that with the kids. Showing videos, reading stories, and having discussions about welcoming people, about being the odd man out, the new person on campus or in the classroom."

Tempest's sister possessed ways of being that also did not align with school expectations, and as a result, she experienced a lack of sociocultural synchronization similar to that observed earlier by Kate. Tempest observed,

> Some kids thrived in the [private Christian school] environment; she [her sister] did not. And so then you get to the traditional, very traditional, classroom where you're at a desk and you keep everything neat, and you must turn in assignments and everything is done the same time for everybody, [and] she didn't do well in that environment. So she was picked on by the kids. They treated her like she was a leper or something. They didn't want to sit at the same table with her and the teachers allowed that kind of behavior and she failed fifth grade. In that process, though [working as the private Catholic school's librarian], I got to see what the school was really like, and I didn't like what I saw.

As in the experiences of the other teachers turned home educators, Tempest's access to the inner workings of the school did not inspire confidence. Her insider perspective led her to believe that the private Christian school she worked in tolerated the norm of not making "outsiders" or new students feel welcomed, or at the very least not making Tempest's sister feel welcomed as a new student. Tempest's attempts to advocate for her sister as an insider failed.

One might presume that teachers whose children attend the school they work in would have an advantage due to their role as an insider within the school community. Such imagined advantages might include the ability to select teachers for their children, or even to secure extra care to meet their needs. However, the mothers featured here did not experience these types of advantages, nor did they trust they would have them.

Though this topic has not been explored in the Black home education literature, it is clear from this research that Black teachers' insider knowledge did not provide them with advantages in their schools. Future research could examine these types of dynamics within homeschool groups.

Interestingly, when they could afford them, Black parents sometimes sought Christian private schools as their first-choice educational context for their children. However, these educational contexts are not necessarily positive for Black children.[16] A social media hashtag, #ExposeChristianSchools, revealed thousands of destructive experiences of alumni and current students attending Christian schools; the tweets "exposed the hypocrisy of religious education institutions that often preach love, peace, and equality while simultaneously offering Biblical and theological justification for slavery, white supremacy, and discrimination."[17] A study of four Black adolescents (seventh and eighth graders) attending a private Christian school in the South found that the students believed their parents thought the Christian school was a better site for their education than public schools, but the students' experiences within the school suggested otherwise.[18] Students described harsh experiences of anti-Blackness that characterized all facets of their schooling experiences, including curriculum, school norms, and interactions with students and teachers. They detailed unfair discipline practices as well as interactions characterized by attempts to perpetuate negative stereotypes and myths of Black people, such as when a teacher insisted that the role of a thief in a play be given to a Black student. Just like the mistreatment of Tempest's sister in her Christian private school, the contradiction between the Bible's teachings and how Black students were treated within this private Christian school was ignored or unnoticed by the adults, including parents. But as a teacher in the school her sister attended, thankfully, Tempest became aware and tried to intervene, but then turned to homeschooling when her interventions failed to stop the pain her sister was experiencing.

Knowledge of Children's Personalities and Abilities

Black teacher-mothers also made decisions to become home educators based on a belief that their children's personalities would cause them to be disproportionately disciplined if they attended traditional schools. Further, they believed that traditional school structures would not be able to address the advanced abilities their children had developed as a result of the teaching they themselves had been doing with them from birth. Teacher-mothers also highlighted distinctions between traditional school contexts and the learning experiences they desired for their children as another factor leading to the decision to home educate. Alayah explained her concern over placing her son in school:

> While he was home, we did the ABCs and everything else so he knew all his letters, all his numbers, the sounds, and was reading small words. I realized that if I put him into a kindergarten class, then he's going to have to do kindergarten stuff unless he gets a teacher who is willing to do the extra work and give him advanced work to align with where he is, and I just couldn't trust that that would

> happen. We decided it would be best if he just stayed home and we kept doing what we were doing. And you don't want to say because it's your child, but he really was way ahead. I taught kindergarten and first grade, so I know what they're doing in those grades.

Recall that earlier, Alayah explained that her insider knowledge led her to believe that getting a "good" teacher for her son was like "a roll of the dice"—too uncertain. This perception contributed to her decision to homeschool her son; she did not want to risk getting a teacher who would be unwilling to continue to push him ahead. Charlise related similar concerns as she described her son reading on the fourth-grade level while he was in first grade.

Alayah also believed that her son's personality would become problematic in traditional school settings. She stated, "With his personality, I knew if we had sent him [to school] he would have been in trouble all the time. I know what he would have been saying to the teachers because when my husband would come home from work, he would say, 'Daddy, Mommy doesn't know any hard work.' So, yeah, picture him in school. Teachers would be like, 'Okay, uh-uh.'" Alayah felt some teachers would not tolerate his unfiltered criticism.

Alayah and Charlise, as well as most of the other Black home educators I have interviewed, were well versed on the issue of discipline disproportionality that plagues Black students' learning experiences. Research has documented that Black children are disciplined more harshly and more frequently than their non-Black counterparts, and that the rate of mistreatment in the South is higher than the national rate.[19] The issue of discipline disproportionality occurs as early as preschool and can stem from teachers' negative bias against Black children.[20] Connections drawn between discipline disproportionality and the school-to-prison pipeline through popular culture outputs such as Ava DuVernay's Netflix documentary simply titled *13th* demonstrate the historical legacy that has contributed to the structurally sanctioned syphoning of Black children from schools into the prison system. The Black mothers in my study who were educators did not believe serving as teachers in their children's schools would provide the professional freedom necessary to protect their children from getting caught up in this system.

Demonstrating a different perspective, Hope came to believe traditional schools would not work for her children after reflecting on her own childhood experiences. She shared, "You know, in the public school where I grew up, everyone stayed on the same page. I saw that when the students worked together, other students could get it quicker than when they worked alone. But as a teacher, I've never had a chance to let them take off into a whole new curriculum at their own pace. But I really liked that idea." Hope's childhood experience with standardized learning did not align with the role she wished to fill as a teacher, as she wanted something better for her own children and for her classroom students. She desired the professional freedom to let her students learn at their own pace. Instead, the district-imposed pacing guide took priority over her professional yearnings. Hope's desired professional freedom included the ability to do more group work because she believed children learned more effectively together than independently. Because Hope concluded that collaboration and flexibility were important aspects of learning for her children, she chose to become a home educator. She did not want her children to be hampered by protocols requiring them to stay on the same level as their peers, if they were ready to move ahead.

Crucially, the challenges of being Black and in traditional schools also influenced former teachers' decisions to homeschool their own children. Kate emphasized,

> I have African American boys, and I think particularly African American boys are often very distanced in school, especially if they're not that typical bright student and they're immediately tagged as being slow or maybe they need to be in special needs class. So having African American boys, I just wanted them to be freer; I wanted them to take the initiative more and be creative and critical thinkers, and I just don't think these are things they necessarily accept even in many private schools. You can't expect that a traditional program will offer them that.

Further describing her sons, Kate shared that one son had a "school personality where he really enjoys the whole institution," which meant that if he continued to want to attend school, she would likely allow him to do so. But she said her "younger son is just such a free spirit, so we'll have to see," and she continued, "I really don't see him being the school type." Here, the concept of the "school type" relates to the notion that traditional schools do not effectively serve students who are nonconformists, or children who would get into trouble for paying attention to their own ideas and ways of doing things rather than remaining in lockstep with teachers' expectations. As already seen in the previous section, Kate's concern could also relate to her knowledge that children who act out or become labeled as troublemakers easily get caught up in special education or the school-to-prison pipeline. The "school type" of student would be a child who follows directions, thrives on structure, remains focused on their work, and generally aims to please the teacher.

TEACHERS' HOME EDUCATION PRACTICE AS FREEDOM PRAXIS

Home education laws differ from state to state, but they all tend to require at least four hours of daily instruction in the foundational subjects of math, reading, science, and social studies/history.[21] The findings from this study, and other research on Black home education, suggests that Black parents who homeschool their children do much more than the laws require. During interviews, Black teacher-moms were asked how they used state curriculum standards, and each of them positioned the grade-level state standards below the content and skills their children were covering in homeschool. In fact, it is not unusual to hear the Black children who are homeschooled have the same realization as Tamara's son, who declared, "Mom, I never did this much work at regular school." To which Tamara responded, "Well, guess what, baby? This isn't regular school."

Indeed, the learning spaces created by Black teachers who became home educators allowed them to teach well beyond the restrictions they experienced as teachers in public and private schools. Further, as depicted in the opening vignette of this chapter, the current climate of teaching in the US also contributed to teachers' decisions to leave their classrooms to homeschool their children. Black home educators' insider knowledge of school climate and culture motivated their decisions to homeschool.

Compared with the schooling experiences they believed their children would have in traditional schools (public and private), choosing to homeschool enabled former teachers to establish learning spaces and an instructional practice that better supported their children's freedom to "be and become." Teacher-mothers' ability to align their professional knowledge with their children's interests and needs represents professional freedom. Their home education practice is a freedom praxis for them as well as their children.

As did nonteacher Black home educators, Black former teachers placed their children at the center of their home educator teaching practice. Their insider knowledge of traditional schools led them to believe that the school's inflexible climate would not meet their children's often advanced academic needs, as well as to believe that their teacher colleagues would not understand or welcome their children's precocious personalities. The study also revealed that Black teachers sometimes experienced discrimination in the form of marginalization and disenfranchisement as they attempted to advocate for or engage in their children's education even within the schools they served in. Black teachers who became home educators witnessed the rigidity of their traditional schools, particularly for Black children, and therefore chose home education for their children. In this way, the experiences of these Black teachers turned home educators corroborate existing literature on the marginalization and disenfranchisement of Black parents as they attempt to advocate for their children within schools.[22] This marginalization and disenfranchisement will be discussed further in the next chapter, which focuses on family engagement directly.

Additionally, scholars have documented the many ways in which traditional schools serve as "sites of suffering" for Black children, which home educators who served as teachers in traditional schools also observed.[23] Moreover, today, seventy years after the passing of the *Brown v. Board of Education* Supreme Court mandate to desegregate schools, US schools continue to suffer from inequity in school funding and segregation.[24] Poor children and children of color attend schools with fewer resources compared with their wealthier and White counterparts.

Black home educators' observations corroborates Michael Dumas's notion that schools are often sites of suffering for Black children.[25] This is particularly true when children's home culture is different from the typical school culture; there is a sociocultural disconnect between these students' home and school lives. Teachers explained that this often results in the students being overlooked or left behind. Charlise personalized it when identifying the reason she chose to homeschool her children: "So we went back to look at these schools, and I knew if I put them in there, they would've been a statistic." This was true for her children and, years later, for the two boys she and her husband adopted. She continued, sharing, "They need a fresh start, and they need someone who is going to work with them." Charlise's insider knowledge led her to believe that once the younger boys' background story got out, the teachers would assume a deficit perspective and expect that her sons would not be able to achieve. But the boys were doing quite well under her homeschool practice.

Home education provides professional freedom for former traditional schoolteachers because they have the time, space, and flexibility to meet their students' needs. Charlise explained, "If my kid doesn't know what three plus three is, I don't need to get upset or yell or become frustrated. Instead, I get three blocks and three more blocks and show them. It might take my child longer to get it, but they get it and then they go, 'Wow, I get it!' and we move on." Charlise further explained that when her oldest son was in a private Christian school, he could quickly recite his addition facts. She said, "I could have just been happy that he knew those facts, but I pushed a bunch of blocks in front of him and I said, 'Show me.' He looked up and said, 'No, just tell me and I can tell you.' I said, 'No, you show me three plus seven is ten.' He said, 'But I just told you it was ten.' He had learned the facts by rote memory, but he could not show me using the blocks.' For Charlise and other Black home educators, her son's inability to demonstrate the concept of "three plus seven equals ten" meant that he really had not *learned* the concept of addition, which was unacceptable. This is an example of what Tempest shared earlier in this chapter about students today being quick to have an answer to give or put on a test but not really understanding the concepts they are discussing. Professional freedom means having the space to ensure that students understand concepts rather than simply asking them to recall facts. Being able to show your work was just as important to these home educators, former teachers, as knowing the facts. As teachers in school, they felt pressured to keep moving through the curriculum and thus could not give students time to be able to show that they understood concepts.

As a teacher educator, I have seen many teachers feel pressured to cover content and keep an instructional pace that they do not get to set themselves; it has been set by someone who is not in a classroom and who does not know the students. The pressure can be so intense that teachers are told what to teach, how to teach it (scripted lessons), and when to teach it. Some districts are run in a way such that teachers are told if it is September 10, ten o'clock in the morning, and you are teaching third grade, an administrator should be able to walk into your classroom, and all other third-grade classrooms, and observe a math lesson on three-digit addition with regrouping being taught. No thought is given to students who might already have mastered three-digit regrouping, or those students who are not yet ready for this lesson because they struggle with the concept of place value. This type of control over teachers' instruction disregards teachers' professional knowledge and competency. It also leads to students being overlooked and left behind because they cannot keep the required pace. Is it any wonder we are facing a teacher shortage, and some Black teachers would choose home education for their own children given these conditions?

LESSONS LEARNED FROM BLACK HOME EDUCATORS: IMPLICATIONS FOR ANYONE AND ANYWHERE

Black teachers' motivations to turn to home education for their own children instead of their traditional schools (public and private) stem from perceived barriers in their workplaces (schools) and motherly duty to seek the best learning environment for their children. Teachers suffer from burnout and anxiety 40 percent more often than health-care workers.[26] Symptoms of teacher burnout and anxiety can include issues related to sleep, appetite, and even hair loss. The list of factors contributing to teachers' anxiety and burnout is long. It includes staff shortages, criticism from parents, low salaries, workload, safety issues, and more. Further, reports indicate that more than half of teachers plan to leave teaching earlier than they initially thought; most teachers (67 percent) feel burnout is a critical issue; and finally, K–12 education represents the field with the highest rate of burnout.[27] Considering these trends and statistics, schools today have become a hazardous workplace for teachers. Under this pressure, anxiety, and fatigue, it is unsurprising that some teachers conclude schools can hardly be optimal sites of learning for their children.

Insights gained from this study and other research indicate that educational leaders would best serve their teachers by generating a culture and climate of respect for the professionalism of educators. Teachers need time and space to get to know their students as human beings and as learners so that they can understand how to most effectively meet their needs. Therefore, this research calls for flexibility that allows teachers to meet these needs rather than emphasizing a pacing guide or scripted lessons. Further, when teachers have children of their own and send them to the school they work in, it sends a powerful message to the community about the value of that school. I often complete recommendation letters for beginning teachers, and there is usually a question that asks, "Would you want this person to teach your children?" Similarly, when evaluating schools, we should ask, Would you send your child here? How do we create schools that teachers want their children to attend? Considering schools as both a workplace and a site of learning, we need to recognize the humanity required to sustain them, and—now more than ever—we should see that relationship building within and outside schools must be a top priority for us all. The remaining chapters of this book will take a deeper look at Black home educators' perspectives on relationship building in the form of parent-teacher partnerships and community building related to teaching and learning.

CHAPTER 5

Parents' Freedom to Choose How to Be Engaged

Portia, a married mother of two sons, decided to homeschool her oldest while her youngest son remained in public school. She explained,

> I volunteer a lot at the school, so I'm at the school a lot, and I listen and watch. Had the teachers been more responsive to [my son's] needs, I would have probably left him there. Starting in fourth grade, that's when it all started. Because he was an honor-roll student, and I was trying to figure out how we went from honor roll to . . . he would make a C. At first, I would say, Cs are unacceptable in my house, but then you realize children are different. Then he made a D in math and reading, and I was like, wait a minute, those are key subjects. If you can't understand when you read, then he'd keep struggling with it and as he gets older it is just a hindrance for him. . . . They [teachers] did a [Child Study Team/special education meeting] starting in the fifth grade. I was looking over the notes from the [Child Study Team], all the different things they were going to do to help. But they weren't doing them! He would go to the [special education resource teacher] for reading and for math. The special reading teacher never had anything positive to say about his progress. Then I felt like it was becoming a crutch for him, that it wasn't motivating him to go to the next level [improve]. We did the [Child Study Team] meeting where different interventions were supposed to be put in place, even in the classroom. Like if he had a low test score, then he could retake the test. Different avenues like that, but they never came to pass.
>
> So we took him out [of school]. I said, "You know what, I'll take responsibility for this because if I don't then that's on me because that's my child and I don't want him to fail. And it wasn't just I don't want him to fail this grade, I don't

want him to fail in learning. Because if this is not taken care of now, it will just keep going on and on and then he'll be frustrated, and I didn't want that. So I just decided that it is not working, and I don't want him to get farther behind.

Family engagement in children's learning has long been associated with increased student achievement.[1] Yet there is a struggle to find a shared definition of family engagement and to determine how much involvement and which types of involvement are appropriate. Overly involved caregivers have been stereotyped as "helicopter parents," while parents who do not participate in parent-teacher conferences are perceived as not caring about their children's education. In the opening vignette, Portia, a stay-at-home mother, shares her perspective on teachers' unresponsiveness to her son's learning needs. Despite her frequent presence in the school and interactions with her oldest son's teachers, Portia did not believe teachers were implementing the strategies they told her they would use to support her son's learning needs. There was a breakdown in the family-school partnership from Portia's perspective. As a result, she and her husband decided to no longer engage in the family-school partnership and to educate their oldest son at home, while his younger sibling remained in school because his needs were being met. To be fair, we do not have the teachers' perspectives on their relationship with Portia and her husband, or on their responsiveness to the child's learning needs. Were they responding to his needs appropriately? Did they dismiss Portia as a helicopter mother? Nonetheless, Portia's actions demonstrate a sense of urgency many parents have in wanting to resolve their children's learning issues. Her example also demonstrates that her first choice was to have her children educated in their local public school, if the family-school partnership had worked well for both of their children. Clearly, when it comes to such partnerships, teachers matter.

Managing parent-teacher relationships can be challenging for teachers. Strong relationships require mutual trust, shared respect, cultural sensitivity, common goals, and open dialogue.[2] However, in 2021 only 51 percent of teacher education programs included at least one course focused on family engagement for preservice teachers.[3] Therefore, many of our nation's educators learn how to partner with parents while on the job rather than in their teacher education programs. Without coursework on developing and maintaining effective family-school partnerships and interactions, educators may take the family-school relationship for granted and repeat common errors. Research and theory on family-school partnerships and interactions have demonstrated that parents and teachers are "natural enemies."[4] When a parent and teacher meet, the parent is typically focused on their child, but the teacher will have the entire classroom of children in mind, which can lead to conflict.[5] This naturally oppositional positioning alone should encourage teacher education programs to place emphasis on parent-teacher relationship building in their pre- and in-service teachers' coursework. Undoubtedly, teachers' limited knowledge and experience regarding the research on family-school partnerships represent an opportunity for improvement.

DEFINING FAMILY ENGAGEMENT

One early conception of family-school partnerships posited that children were at the center of three conceptual overlapping Venn diagram circles, representing home, school, and community, and that adults in all three contexts collaborated to support children's learning.[6] This model became the foundational definition of parental involvement and family-school-community partnerships for the National Parent Teacher Association and highly influenced research. Other scholars have further suggested that family-school partnerships require stakeholders (e.g., teachers, students, and parents) to engage in mutual trust, interdependence, and vulnerability to establish a collective trust.[7] Moreover, the parental role construction model presented factors that inform parents' decisions on how to be engaged in their children's education.[8] The model included factors such as parents' self-efficacy and parents' motivations. But it did not consider the role parents' emotions play in determining how they will be involved in their children's education, which research has found serves as a foundational motivation for Black parents who decide to assume full control over their children's education through homeschooling.[9] Similarly, the collective trust model and the overlapping spheres model failed to consider the perspectives of racially, culturally, or linguistically diverse families. Instead, these conceptions of parental involvement assumed a White middle-class perspective, and they also assumed a school-centric perspective rather than recognizing parents' sovereignty in their engagement decision-making.

In this book, parental involvement has been conceptualized as a key feature in Black parents' pursuit of educational justice for their children. In other words, Black parents' decisions regarding how they will be involved in their children's education mediate their role as child privacy protectors in preserving their children's freedom "to be and become," which this book employs as a conceptual frame for educational justice.[10] Centering this work in educational justice requires us to honor parents' right to choose how and when they will engage in their children's education. This includes parents' decisions to not engage in ways that school staff expect or need. Research that narrowly defines parental involvement and parental engagement ignores parents' daily practices of agency and self-determination on behalf of their children's education outside the school. When considering the parental involvement choices of Black parents, we must consider the actions they take to combat and overcome continuing false discourse on the inferiority of Black people, deficit thinking about Black families, and the damaging conditions of Black home education that have led to the notion of schools as "sites of suffering" for Black children.[11] Therefore, this work recognizes what parents do on a daily basis to be involved and engaged in their children's education, rather than focusing on the actions they may take within, or in support of, traditional schools. As theorized by Najarian Peters, these parental actions fall into categories such as safeguarding Black childhood, giving Black children the opportunity to direct their own lives, and shielding Black children from damaging images and portrayals of Black people.[12]

Therefore, this chapter presents Black parents' perspectives on family-school partnerships and interactions. Specifically, it addresses the question, What lessons can be learned by examining Black parents' perspectives on their relationships with teachers and administrators before they chose to home educate? The chapter moves beyond my own studies of Black home educators to present research on how Black parents experience the family-school partnership and offers insights for scholars and teacher educators to aid in understanding how to engage parents effectively given diverse cultural, linguistic, and racial backgrounds.

BLACK PARENTING AND BLACK PARENTS IN PARENT-TEACHER RELATIONSHIPS

In this section, I provide a review of the literature with a particular focus on key components of family-school partnerships and interactions, as well as Black parent marginalization and disenfranchisement. Additionally, I provide examples of findings from the more recent research on Black home education, which corroborates the existing scholarship on Black parents' family-school interactions.

Note that I have intentionally selected key studies that refute long-standing myths and stereotypes regarding Black parents, Black mothers in particular. Some of the articles may seem dated, but this does not negate the value of the findings; instead, it enables us to acknowledge the generations of Black parents who have had to endure challenges and barriers to involvement in their children's education. The work also provides much-needed counternarratives that present Black parents' perspectives on parental involvement and engagement. For these reasons, this section privileges research that has highlighted the voices and experiences of Black parents. Moreover, this review of the literature focuses primarily on Black mothers, not because Black fathers are absent, but because in the Black community, Black mothers tend to be the ones who participate in the research, sharing their experiences and beliefs regarding their children's education. In other spaces, research focused on Black mothers has been devalued because it is deemed too impressionistic and overly emotional.[13] However, such critiques do not consider that child privacy laws in this country give us the freedom "to be and become," which Black parents enact when they choose to homeschool their children.[14] As privacy protectors, a role that is the basis of educational freedom within this text, home educators preserve their children's right to an education free from racism, prejudice, and bias. Yes, it is emotional. We are talking about mothers and their children; how could it not be emotional? In fact, as discussed earlier, one of the issues with current conceptions of parental engagement is that we ignore the emotional motivations of parents' decisions regarding participating in their children's education.[15] Moreover, only someone who has not read the existing literature on Black motherhood, does not understand it, or has an anti-Black stance could describe the literature as lacking in intellectualism. The increasing amount of research on Black motherhood shows institutional support for the work as well. "*Mother* is the first institution of life and knowledge" and therefore worthy of exploration.[16] Like a recent special issue of *Urban Education* that focused on Black mothers, this book mines Black mothers' everyday epistemology and pedagogy to inform teacher education and practices in traditional schools for Black children and for all children.

"PARENTING WHILE BLACK"

If you search the internet for the phrase "parenting while Black," you will find it has been used in discussions of specific issues related to Black mothers in childbirth, in seminars and workshops for Black parents, as parental conference themes, in legal forums, and in titles of scholarly works. "Parenting while Black" is a concept in and of itself that needs to be addressed before diving into findings from family-school partnership research.

Media reports of Black youth being gunned down by police have become an all-too-common occurrence.[17] Low student achievement based on test scores among Black students has been a persistent issue in our schools.[18] Successful birth rates for Black mothers are lower in the US compared with almost any other nation.[19] Black bodies are surveilled to the extent that we must teach our children not to put their hands in their pockets while in stores. The school-to-prison pipeline targets Black and Brown children. Today, Black parents must help their children navigate successfully in a world full of anti-Blackness within and outside schools. Anti-Blackness is all encompassing and has an impact on our physical and mental wellness; it is hard to escape. Research has begun to capture the ways race and racism inform Black mothers' roles as protectors of their children and as resistors of the racism their children face daily.[20] Additionally, research has revealed that having a middle-class to high socioeconomic status does not enable us to overcome anti-Blackness within or outside schools. Middle-class Black parents have expressed feeling intimidated in school spaces intended to support parent-teacher collaboration to meet children's special education needs.[21] As sociologist Dawn Marie Dow notes, "Despite being middle- and upper-middle class, and thus having more resources than their lower-income counterparts, these mothers felt limited in their abilities to protect their sons and daughters from the challenges associated with being African American boys (and future men) and girls (and future women)."[22] As Black parents, we tend to understand that schools were not initially intended for us or our children, which means we must help our children navigate and attempt to thrive in spaces based in damaging structures and systems not designed to meet our needs.[23]

Scholars have further documented the significance of racial identity, trust, and student outcomes within the family-school relationship.[24] From this work we know that having a strong racial identity, or positive sense of one's racial identity, can lead to strong parental agency on behalf of our children.[25] However, one study also found that some middle-class Black parents seek good-quality schools for their children and then take a hands-off approach to their engagement at the school, assuming all is well. In contrast, a parent who participated in that study offered, "Many people don't think we [African Americans] belong here [in suburban communities], so we need to be on top of our kids to do right, and then to make sure we have cultural events for our kids. Make sure that they have access to Gifted and Talented Education, AP classes, college curriculum. That's what we need to do."[26] Yet research has also demonstrated that parents, including Black parents, often lack the information needed to effectively advocate on their children's behalf.[27] Our racial identity colors our decision-making related to our children's education and has a formidable influence over our children's outcomes.[28] This is critical to consider in today's context. Imagine being a Black parent living in one of the states that recently banned the terms *diversity*, *equity*, and *inclusion* from their educational standards, or in Florida, where courses on AP African American studies have been called into question and banned.[29] As a relatively communal culture, our community steps in to overcome and resist such hurdles on behalf of our children; Black churches in Florida started teaching African American history when the schools banned the topic.[30]

Furthermore, being a single Black mother also comes with all kinds of negative stereotypes.[31] Early in my career, I attended a talk by a state dignitary who was a Black male. In his talk, he discussed some of the challenges the state was facing. At one point, he stated, "Single-parent homes, we all know they cannot raise a family; they are broken." As a single mother, I wanted to stand up and call him a liar. How dare he make such a broad-stroke, slanderous assumption about single-parent households! Painful life experiences such as this, and having a neighbor call me a part-time mother because I was working on a doctoral degree full time, have taught me that many people see my family as broken, or problematic in some other way, just because I am a single mom. For this reason, my first book focused on single Black mothers who homeschooled their children full time without working full time.[32] Single-parent households are families; we are not broken. To continue to frame us as broken perpetuates false narratives and enables society to ignore our strengths.

Patricia Hill Collins's pivotal work in Black feminist thought acknowledges stereotypes of Black women as Jezebels/whores, matriarchs, welfare queens, mammies, and Sapphires (angry Black women).[33] She explains that these negative conceptions of Black women permeate all aspects of society, and Black women fight against them daily to challenge and resist these long-standing false narratives about Black women. Melissa Harris-Perry's notion of the "crooked room" also serves as a framework for understanding the challenges and complexity of being a Black woman in America.[34] She builds on Collins's work by demonstrating that the negative stereotypes ascribed to Black women can alter our perception of ourselves and how we navigate society such that we perceive the world around us as a straight or upright room, but ourselves as tilted; it is as though we are trying to stand up in a crooked room but we cannot see that it is the room that is crooked, not us.[35] Our attempts to stand straight represent the resilience of Black women as they resist the caricatures society has perpetuated for centuries.

Robin Lenhardt, a legal scholar, writes, "In deploying the term 'parenting while Black,' I mean to invoke not only the criminal justice context, but also all the systems that inform the functioning and well-being of families of color. Enumerating such systems provides us with a deeper appreciation of the obstacles that parents of color must navigate in trying to provide for their children."[36] Similarly, to truly comprehend the challenges Black parents face, we must understand that anti-Blackness is institutionally and individually perpetuated, whether intentionally or unintentionally.

STEREOTYPES AND BIAS

Black mothers are aware of how teachers negatively perceived them. Camille Wilson Cooper's research with fourteen Black mothers who self-reported their low-income or working-class status revealed, "Most mothers associated educators' bias with the negative opinions they held about their children's racial background, disability, or single-parent households."[37] Contrary to the myth of Black parents' disinterest in their children's education, Cooper's work documented low-income Black mothers' engagement in and concern regarding their children's education through school choice options. The study showed that when teachers expressed deficit thinking about Black children's ability and potential, Black parents exercised their right to choose a different school, seeking more positive settings for their children's learning and better concern and care for their children's overall well-being. Further, mothers took the time to research school settings before choosing them for their children. Black mothers navigated the school system to the best of their ability. Often,

> the mothers perceived their [neighborhood] schools as unsafe and having poor academics and/or inappropriate special education programs for their children. The

> three mothers [out of fourteen] who have children with special needs explained that they were aware of open enrollment policies and their right to select a school that could accommodate their children. They gained this awareness by educating themselves about their children's rights. These mothers agreed that obtaining information about their school choice options via word-of-mouth is often easier than getting it from district officials. . . . While the Walker [Middle School] and Hillsdale [Charter School] mothers have learned to take advantage of the public school choice policies, they agreed that unlike White affluent parents in LAUSD [the Los Angeles Unified School District], they lack adequate information about their options, for which they blame the district. So again, the mothers pointed to their race and class as being aspects of their positionality that disadvantage them when choosing schools.[38]

Cooper's work demonstrates low-income Black mothers' approaches to evaluating the quality of school settings (public and private) before enrolling their children. Participating mothers in this seminal study had a keen awareness of the contradictory role of vouchers, which they believed served very few Black families and ultimately took much-needed funding from public education. Additional research by Cooper has effectively demonstrated the ways in which school personnel can view Black mothers' approach to caring for their children from a deficit perspective.[39] This work illustrates how the deficit perspectives of school staff that are applied to Black mothers who do not "act" in ways teachers deem acceptable correlate with negative stereotypes and myths about Black mothers identified in Collins's Black feminist thought. When Black mothers recount their attempts to partner with their children's teachers, they often describe having to contend with teachers' low expectations for their children or teachers' contemptuous attitudes and racial bias toward them as they try to advocate for their children.[40]

Black mothers are also aware of the anti-Blackness and bias their children experience in schools. A published letter from a Black mom to her son, who was less than two years old, includes the following message:

> Before I know it, Caleb, you will be throwing your backpack on and waving goodbye as you run off across the playground. I think about that moment often and wonder about the condition of the schools you'll enter. I worry about sending you, my Black son, to schools that over-enroll Black boys into special education, criminalize them at younger and younger ages, and view them as negative statistics on the dark side of the achievement gap.[41]

In the letter, the mother describes her experiences of feeling invisible and isolated as a Black child in an integrated school. Then she writes to her son,

> Caleb, I want your teachers to help you love being in your skin. I want them to make space for you in their curricula, so that you see yourself as integral to this country's history, to your classroom's community, to your peers' learning. I want your teachers to select materials where Blacks are portrayed in ordinary and extraordinary ways that actively challenge stereotypes and biases. Most of all, Caleb, I want your teachers to know you so they can help you to grow.[42]

The letter continues with more hopes and dreams for Caleb's teachers throughout his educational journey. What strikes me most about this letter is that this mom is hoping that his teachers will see her son as a human being, as a learner, and as a positive member of the classroom community. She is hoping his teachers will help him grow as a human being and in knowledge. She is also hoping that Caleb will not be seen in comparison to racial stereotypes, myths, or bias, but as he is. Given that teaching is a professional field, this seems like so little to ask of an educator. Yet the research tells us otherwise. The learning environment this mother hopes and dreams of for her son is not readily available to Black children.

Unfortunately, the anti-Blackness, school-to-prison pipeline, and all other forms of Black suffering in schools begin early. Recently, a two-year-old I know was suspended from his private preschool for "showing his private parts to the girls." Now, I ask you, does a two-year-old typically think in a sexual manner? I think not! On further exploration, I discovered that when the young man is playing outside at home and he must go to the bathroom, the family tells him to go in the bushes instead of going back in the house. Whatever you think about this, this is what the family does while enjoying time outside on their property. So, naturally, while playing at recess, when the young man had to go to the bathroom, he found a tree or bush and did what he does at home. He is still learning about social decorum. He does not know this is not an "appropriate" thing to do at school. If there are girls near the area he decides to go, at two, he feels free (as he should) to go like he goes at home. Why did the preschool teachers sexualize this incident? I share this account with you to demonstrate how easily and quickly Black children become labeled as "problems" even under innocent conditions. When this young man's mother explained to him that he should only go to the bathroom outside at home, he understood instantly and said, "Thank you for telling me, Mommy." Children are far more capable of understanding when we just take the time to talk with them instead of throwing them out of the classroom or out of school. Teachers who operate out of fear or based on stereotypes, myths, and biases are dangerous to Black children.

Research on Black homeschooling has further demonstrated Black mothers' experiences with negative stereotypes, myths, and biases in family-school interactions. In many cases, Black parents choose homeschooling as a way of overcoming or avoiding the negative perspectives of Black children harbored by many school personnel. For example, in the previous chapter, Charlise shared that she and her husband decided to homeschool in part to keep their children from becoming statistics, meaning they wanted them to avoid the negative experiences associated with being Black and in schools. Even parents who homeschooled from birth indicated that stereotypes and biases related to being Black and anti-Black sentiments informed their decision. Monica, a veteran home educator of three sons, shared, "My husband's theory is that if they [their sons] started to go to school, they'd become aware of how the world sees them, and that the world sees them as not being high achievers and that affects them, my boys. I think we've been able to not have our boys really deal with those issues by homeschooling." Whether experienced directly or perceived as a possibility, bias and stereotypes influence Black parents' determination to homeschool.

DISENFRANCHISEMENT AND MARGINALIZATION OF BLACK PARENTS

Parental involvement has become an expected, normed practice that determines the appropriateness of parents' actions within schools.[43] In many schools, the parental involvement norms promote unity and power among those with similar values by encouraging involvement practices typically associated with White middle-class mothers (e.g., volunteering, fundraising, and chaperoning).[44] However, these parental involvement standards also marginalize parents whose involvement practices differ from school norms. Most often, low-income or working-class and linguistically or culturally diverse families experience this marginalization. Parental involvement research and practice have tended to emphasize a school-based perspective; therefore, as Fabienne Doucet describes, "within the system, parents whose life circumstances and work schedules do not permit them to volunteer during school hours, or otherwise participant within the constraints of the school's goals and needs, are, de facto, excluded from school."[45] The researcher's work with Haitian immigrant families documents the ways in which cultural differences in gender roles within the home and cultural capital led to marginalization.[46] Other research has contributed to our understanding of how structural barriers have led to culturally and linguistically diverse parents' marginalization and disenfranchisement from full, equitable engagement in their children's education.[47]

Black home education research has revealed evidence of the marginalization and disenfranchisement of parents as well. Previously published research and memoirs all describe barriers Black parents have faced in public and private schools as they attempted to advocate for their children. Paula Penn-Nabrit, who homeschooled her boys into top higher education institutions, described failed attempts to advocate for more rigorous learning opportunities for her sons in a private school. Moreover, though she actively participated on the private school's diversity committee, her advocacy for Black male representation on the school staff fell on deaf ears. Multiple concerns motivated Penn-Nabrit's advocacy in this area, including the fact that the lack of Black male representation on the school staff perpetuated the "myth of the exceptional Negro," which could lead to internalized racism in Black children.[48] The author explains,

> The diversity coordinator listened attentively and then explained that the issues of gender were more important because people can, with enough money, escape the challenge of racial diversity thereby making it an elective, while the issue of gender is inescapable, thereby making it mandatory. While I thought the analysis was grossly oversimplified and I vehemently disagreed with it, I felt enlightened by our conversation. As a Black woman with Black sons, I knew the school would place the needs of White girls ahead of those of Black boys. The Diversity coordinator knew that too; it's just that that wasn't really a problem for her.[49]

The author further discloses that she intentionally aimed to communicate in such meetings in nonthreatening ways in order to be heard, yet she was not heard. Though she participated within the school, the like-minded, majority-White parents remained united against the ideas presented by Black parents and they maintained decision-making power. The following year, Penn-Nabrit did what we typically do when we are denied access, which is to build a coalition. She organized an "unofficial" picnic for Black families with children who attended the private school. The attending Black parents began talking about building a network and engaging in collective advocacy on behalf of their children. Shortly after the event, the school's headmaster called Penn-Nabrit to his office; surprisingly, or maybe not surprisingly, he had found out about the picnic because some Black parents were angry about having been invited to the "Black" picnic, as they apparently did not want to be included in events that emphasized their racial identity. The headmaster was angry with Penn-Nabrit, and by the end of that week, her sons had been expelled from the school. It doesn't matter why, but you can read the book if you are interested. This incident from the memoir illustrates the fact that Black people are not monolithic, and some Black families can be communal, especially when it comes to advocacy on behalf of our children. But the school staff and parents who held power within this school did not welcome Penn-Nabrit's attempts to coalesce Black parents, though it would have helped the school embody its self-proclaimed commitment to diversity in more sincere ways than the school's diversity committee. This school and others like it have commitments to diversity as long as to do so does not take resources away from White children's educational needs. If Black parents want to meet their children's needs and help them develop a positive racial identity, we often must take action outside school, including through home education.

Patterns of disenfranchisement and marginalization persist throughout the research literature on Black home education. When Dahlia, a Black single mother, pulled her son out of a well-resourced elementary school (over thirty minutes from their home in the same district) that they both loved to support a predominantly Black new charter school coming to their neighborhood, she had hoped for a culturally relevant, rigorous, and joyful learning experience for her child.[50] But when the charter school failed two years later, the district would not allow her to re-enroll in the school they had left and she was forced to find a school in her underresourced, resegregated section of the district. Not thinking about home education, she enrolled her son in two other public schools, where he experienced low teacher expectations, damage to his self-esteem, and a loss of the joy of learning until Dahlia finally made the decision to homeschool him as a last resort. Her account reminds us of the inequity in school choice, in-district school resource inequity, and the power of Black parents' perseverance to find or create educational excellence for their children.

Critical work has been conducted that substantiates the idea that Black home education enacts various forms of parental protection.[51] This work explicitly demonstrates Black parents' role as racial protectionists. It documents the ways Black parents, in addition to protecting their children from racism outside the school, must also protect them from teachers' racialized actions. Ama Mazama and Garvey Lundy explain, "Teachers were commonly described as being unresponsive and overly critical of Black children, mean to them, unsupportive, unwilling or unable to show compassion and patience, abusing their authority, and treating Black children like animals."[52] As described in the opening vignette in this chapter, Portia experienced such unresponsiveness from teachers. Teachers say things to parents like, "When she wants to learn, she will learn," as if this were a benign statement.[53] But parents interpret this as a lack of care on the part of teachers. Similarly, Yvette, whom I interviewed in an earlier study, allowed her son to be tested by the school because she believed he was acting out in school because the work he had been given represented content he already knew.[54] But when the results showed that he was performing above grade level, the teacher chose to continue to focus on his "negative" behavior instead of providing more advanced work. We cannot say for sure what the teacher was thinking in making this decision not to listen to the mother or place value on the test results, but Yvette interpreted it as a lack of responsiveness and as an educational and emotional assault on her son. Research indicates that Black parents who choose to home educate in order to protect their children from such assaults also engage in other forms of protectionism, such as protecting Black children's spiritual and religious well-being, specifically focusing on Black boys' needs, making cultural connections in the curriculum, and ensuring a quality education.[55]

I could continue with this review of Black home education literature because, thankfully, the research is growing. However, there are still areas to be explored. For example, to date, only one study has focused on the experiences of rural Black home educators.[56] The research showed that Black home educators in rural areas can experience racial and political isolation. Interestingly, it also demonstrates that tremendous diversity exists in how we define and experience rurality. Though the body of literature is certainly growing, the field has scarcely begun to capture the wide variety of Black home education practices. What remains clear from the existing research is that Black parents' decisions to homeschool typically stem from negative racialized experiences within traditional schools, intentional or perceived. Black parents also choose homeschooling because, contrary to the long-standing myths, they do care about their children's education, and they seek the best for them. My research on Black home education reinforces the existing empirical studies of issues in Black home education, including parental involvement and engagement.

RECOGNIZING PARENTS' FREEDOM TO CHOOSE HOW TO BE INVOLVED

The overriding lesson learned from Black parents' courageous decisions to homeschool their children is that parents, all parents, have the right to choose how to be involved in their children's learning. Honoring parents' freedom to choose their involvement approach in our research and teaching represents a starting point toward creating educational justice for parents, and ultimately children. In this section, I share ideas on what this paradigm means for research and in the practice of teaching.

Embracing Parents' Freedom and Other Lessons Learned from Research

The lessons learned from research with Black home educators, and other Black parents, indicate a need to employ theoretical and conceptual frameworks that support parents' right and freedom to choose if and how they will engage in their children's education. Rather than succumbing to old ways of conceptualizing parental involvement and engagement, researchers can honor parents' freedom to decide how to engage by employing conceptual frameworks such as the Ecologies of Parental Engagement (EPE).[57] The EPE framework recognizes and values the ways parents engage in their children's education outside school, including within their homes and throughout the community. Conceptualizing parental engagement in this manner effectively broadens the definition of what counts as parental engagement activity well beyond the traditional school-based parental involvement activities. Further, the EPE framework includes a focus on equity and power sharing in the family-school relationship via application of critical race theory and social capital theory. Finally, the EPE framework also engages analysis in the history of relationships within a community, how decisions have been made in that space, and collective interaction over time. This type of expansive definition of parental involvement and engagement is essential to understanding the full power of parents to determine how they want to participate in their children's education, even if they decide not to be fully engaged.[58]

Thankfully, today's family engagement scholars have many interdisciplinary theoretical and conceptual frameworks to choose from to honor Black parents' freedom. For example, critical parental engagement blends critical race theory with the psychologically based critical consciousness theory that emphasizes how Black parents experience the inequity and racism their children, or they, experience, and how they decide to respond to those experiences.[59] These conceptual frameworks are essential for Black family-school relationship research because they consider the racialized context in which Black parents have had to engage historically and today.[60] Given the strong connection between racial identity and Black parents' decisions to be engaged that is identified in the literature discussed earlier, understanding Black parents' engagement warrants such frameworks. It would also follow that similar culturally responsive frameworks should be used when researching the engagement practices of other culturally, linguistically, and racially diverse parents.

Black families are diverse in their views on how, and even if, they should be engaged in their children's education. Throughout the literature review and this text, Black parents have expressed diverging views on their motivations to homeschool and how they approach their home education. The same is true for how Black parents decide to engage in their children's education within traditional schools. Using conceptual frameworks that broaden the definition of parental engagement and involvement will help to capture the variances among families.

Moreover, in the past twenty years, my research methodology has become increasingly culturally responsive as I (re)learned and gain self-efficacy in using methods tied to Black women's ways of being and reflective of our communal and spiritual sense of being.[61] This has been a journey of deprioritizing positivistic and individualistic approaches to research that do not align with Black women's values, and learning that it is not only "okay" but also necessary that I embrace who I am within my research.

The journey began with diving deeply into African American educational history and finally learning the truth about our legacy of excellence in education that occurred in segregated Black schools, as well as before them.[62] This is the opposite of what I learned in all my education in K–12, college, and a master's program in elementary education. Learning the truth about our educational legacy included realizing the integral role of community in supporting Black children's learning, as well as the roles of parents and Othermothers.[63] Further, Black feminist thought and endarkened feminist epistemology, which emphasize the value of Black women's daily living as ways of knowing, empowered me to rethink what counts as research and how to approach research with Black women, not research on them.

My research design, methods, and conceptual stance became increasingly culturally relevant as I engaged readings written by and for Black women. For example, instead of focus groups, I employed Sister Circles.[64] The difference was that the research emphasized relationship building and the participating mothers determined the direction of the research more than I did. I assumed the position of a member of the circle. Reciprocity has also played a major role in the research I have conducted over the years. Overall, as I learned more about my history as a Black woman in educational research and began to understand the families I do research with, I observed how much more culturally congruent my work became. In the midst of this journey, I visited Ghana, West Africa, three times, which also had a profound impact on my learning to relate my work to our ancestral ways of knowing.[65]

To be culturally responsive in our research, we must first understand who we are, including our ancestral heritage, and we must spend time building relationships with participants in ways that positivistic approaches do not usually honor. This is especially true for qualitative research. But scholars are beginning to talk about the need for culturally responsive quantitative work in Black home education as well.[66]

Recognizing Parents' Freedom to Choose in Educational Practice

As discussed in the introduction of this chapter, teacher education programs frequently do not include coursework that focuses on educators' role in the family-school relationship. In this section, I share theoretical and research-based ideas I have used as a teacher educator to prepare pre- and in-service teachers to develop a family engagement philosophy and practice.

Instruction in family-school-community partnerships gives pre- and in-service educators an opportunity to identify their biases, develop a practice of building connections between home and children's learning, and enhance their ability to cultivate effective relationships with parents. Self-reflection is the starting place for implementing major theories such as culturally relevant pedagogy, culturally sustaining pedagogy, culturally responsive pedagogy, and multicultural education. Before we can understand others, we must understand our biases. In this way, including a focus on family-school relationships can benefit all types of teacher-parent relationships.

We all must understand that cultural differences are not always racial differences. For example, some families lean toward being individualistic, while others are more communal.[67] Influenced by research in this area, as an exercise in class, I ask my students, "How many of you grew up with your own room and having your own closet space without having to share?" Whereas some children have their own space at home, in communal homes, children may not have such space, and everything is shared. What are the types of conflicts that may arise in a classroom when children with these different types of cultural homeplaces interact? How can we handle these conflicts in a way that would promote cultural understanding rather than punishing children? How might we anticipate such cultural differences in the way we set up our classroom spaces, routines, and procedures so that children of all cultural backgrounds can feel welcome?

Anticipating Family-Teacher Conflict

The research is clear: conflict between parents and teachers/schools is inevitable, and this conflict can bring about positive change within schools if handled well.[68] Therefore, anything we can do to dispel pre- and in-service teachers' apprehension in working with parents would be quite helpful in teacher education. Thus, instruction in parent-teacher relationships should include preparing in-service and preservice teachers to anticipate and address conflict.

When I teach about family-school relationships, I use blinded excerpts from my research, vignettes created from my research, and publications authored by teachers describing how they engage parents. As a local example, I use the work of a doctoral alum of our program who turned her dissertation into a book titled *Teaching Through the Storm: A Journal of Hope.*[69] In a chapter titled "A Stormy Beginning," our former student, Karen, describes in tremendous detail her initial meeting with a Black mother. The meeting took place in the early evening hours when the school was rather empty. Karen wrote in her journal entry about that day,

> I was somewhat distracted by the lateness of the hour, by wondering about my own family, and by the depth of tiredness that always accompanies the opening of school. I slowed my banter, tried to make eye contact, and said, "Well . . . what specifically did you want to meet about today?"
>
> She clinched her purse in her hands, continued to stare out the window, and nearly whispered, "Look . . . I never met you, I don't even know your name. But

> you are my enemy. I hate you and everybody connected to this school and any other school for what you are trying to do to my baby, my precious child."
>
> Her anger was palpable, breathtaking. As she continued her accusations toward me and schools it was hard for me to know for certain whether my inability to breathe came from her consumption of the very air available in that room or from my holding my breath in a survival mode.
>
> She was clutching her purse, release, pat, clutch, release, pat. I felt her anger growing at least as fast as my fear.[70]

When I use this excerpt in my teacher education courses, I end it at this point and ask my pre- or in-service educators, What would you do or say next and why? After we discuss our choices, I share with them how Karen responded, which leads to even further discussion. What is important here is a focus on humanity, not defending against the specific accusations this mother made. Instead, Karen responded in a way that recognized this mother's pain, and more than anything, Karen listened. She took the necessary steps to begin to repair the harm of others, and to build trust and an authentic partnership with this mother.

This is a great example of humanizing our relationships with parents. Instead of focusing on her fear, Karen took the time to listen and to see this mother's pain. For Karen, it was mother to mother. But teachers do not have to be mothers to empathize with the parents of the children they teach. They just need to take a moment to look beyond themselves and listen. In addition to *Teaching Through the Storm*, I create vignettes from real-life encounters I had with parents when I was a teacher, examples from other educators' experiences with parents, situations found in my raw data, and even incidents that happened while my students were in their field practicums (though changing the names of people and places). If we spend time with educators or listen to parents sharing about their in-school experiences, we will hear accounts of real-life parent-teacher relationships to use as vignettes. Accounts from both sides, teachers' and parents', help pre- and in-service teachers practice engaging with families. Vignettes can spur role-play, which can further equip teacher education students in developing their responses to unexpected encounters with parents.

Finally, teacher education can create spaces where students meet parents of all types to discuss family engagement. I have done this numerous times in my courses, and I am always amazed by the diverse perspectives that emerge among a small panel of parents. For example, during a panel with four parents, one of my students ask how they felt about teacher home visits. One parent had experienced a home visit from a teacher and found it to be a wonderful experience for the entire family because it built a bond with their children's teacher. Two of the other parents had not experienced a home visit from a teacher but expressed an openness to doing so. But the one father on the panel vehemently expressed disgust regarding the idea of having a teacher visit his home. He could not see the purpose or need for such a visit. These differences in responses to home visits were quite helpful—they allowed my students to see the importance of valuing the uniqueness of each family rather than assuming all families will welcome the same type of engagement from them as their children's teachers.

Employing the Village

From the research, we know that even when school leaders intentionally seek and implement practices intended to broaden parents' involvement roles and to promote increased inclusion of diverse parental perspectives, "assumptions, attitudes, and behaviors that are played out by human actors and established institutional norms" marginalize the voices of linguistically and culturally diverse parents.[71] This happens intentionally or unintentionally, and usually among Black parents. For example, maybe a parent who is somewhat new to the PTA/PTO attends a meeting and offers an idea, and parents in leadership roles on the PTA/PTO respond, "We don't do that here," or "In the past . . ." This response can sometimes serve as a barrier to new parents' participation. Some type of intervention is needed to keep the line of communication open and, on the flip side, to keep parents' power in check. In other words, we need parents and teachers to be committed to equity and inclusion in order to ensure the dialogue and decision-making remain open to all.

It really does take a village to educate children. We need those parents who have the time and willingness to serve as parent leaders. But we also need parents of all types to share ideas to keep parental engagement innovative and friendly in order to have a strong school community. School leaders and teachers should be aware of cultural brokers and fictive kinfolk within the school community who can help keep dialogue focused on what is best for the children and the school.

Cultural brokers function like liaisons on behalf of individual children, specific groups of children, or the entire school.[72] I have experienced parents, school staff members, and teachers serving as cultural brokers within the schools that I taught in. Cultural brokers can help schools connect meaningfully with culturally and linguistically diverse communities.[73] They can be hired staff. For example, in the community I live in, our school district has parent coordinators. Some of the people serving in this role have intimate knowledge of the school community and help connect families to the school or their children's learning experience in ways that teachers may not be able to given time and other constraints.

Similarly, fictive kinfolk within school communities can help bridge the gap between families and schools.[74] Fictive kinfolk are people who assume family-like roles with others. Among the Black community, fictive kinfolk are commonly referred to as our "play" moms, dads, aunts, brothers, or sisters. "Play" indicates that the relationship is not a blood relationship but instead is chosen.[75] The idea of fictive kinfolk is decades old, but I could only locate research that documents the role fictive kinfolk play in the lives of high school and college students, which notes that they sustain students' motivation and focus on their education and encourage other successful outcomes. Less is known, research-wise, about the role of fictive kinfolk in the lives of elementary children and early adolescents. The next chapter focuses on the role of community in the educational lives of Black children, and I will dive more deeply into both cultural brokers and fictive kinfolk there.

Combining Research and Teacher Education

When researchers conduct community-based research projects with families and teacher education students, they create spaces where everyone benefits. Such research has the capacity to bring together families, educators, and curriculum. As an example, two former colleagues conducted community workshops with Latino families in science education, which also informed teacher education practice.[76] This National Science Foundation–funded research project bridged gaps between science curriculum content and families' funds of knowledge to enhance students' learning. Moreover, doctoral students who were emerging teacher educators at the time collaborated in the research, learning how to design and implement research that serves school communities in meaningful ways. This project has contributed to our understanding of Latino family interactions and more. Along these same lines, community-based research projects in partnership with school districts have the capacity to enhance initial certification teachers' understanding of family engagement, student learning, and community culture while also supporting student learning. The next chapter will dive more deeply into these possibilities through a focus on the role of community in family-school relationships.

Overall, acknowledging parents' right to choose their form of engagement in their children's schooling helps ensure that we will respect them and honor them as their children's first teachers, rather than requiring that they meet our expectations. Holding on to our assumptions about parents prevents us from hearing and understanding their perspectives. By honoring parents' freedom to decide how to engage, we support trust building between teachers and parents. Parents are our path toward getting to know our students, and parents rely on us to provide the best learning experiences we can give their children. We need one another to do our jobs effectively. Yet while we are building mutual trust, we must also expect that miscommunication or differences of opinion will likely occur. This creates a pathway to focus on humanity, but as educators we must also remain professional. Collaborating with parents can ease some of the challenges we face as educators. Additionally, as research finds ways to combine school-based and community-based service-oriented projects, we can learn more about the strengths and challenges in collaborating with families.

CHAPTER 6

Ubuntu and the Power of Community

Here is an excerpt from one of my interviews with Alana, a home education leader and veteran home educator:

ALANA: So one of the things that I believe is that we do not have the right to call together a group of people and say we are starting a program, if we are not willing to steward community.

CHERYL: Hmm! Good point! Tell me some more about what you mean by that.

A: So that means that we have to teach people how to get along with each other. We have to be willing to create environments to support parents. We have to be willing to teach people about conflict resolution, we have to be willing to talk about what bullying is and what it looks like. 'Cause a lot of times people come in and we just assume, "Okay, we called you here. We have a program!" and that we just need to teach our classes and that's it. But there's just so much to this. We have to become mentors to parents and to the students. If you're not willing to do all of that, [*slight pause*] then don't open a program. Because what you will be doing is calling people into chaos and more hurt.

Later in the interview, Alana described how her homeschool group resolved an issue with single parents getting their children to the program.

A: We don't want kids left at home. That's one of the dangers that I see with this homeschooling thing expanding is people knowing their kids need something different. Some kids, like, they are not going to live [thrive] if they stay in the traditional environment they are in right now because of bullying, or their own struggles that they are going through. And so parents know that they have to do something different, but because they don't have the extra support, that child ends up being at home by themself and that is not good.

So we get involved, we end up in the lives of people. We have kids who are depressed. There might be someone who is suicidal. So sometimes we have called in someone else. You know, we don't have the expertise to handle this. So there are people on staff here at the church, which is another part of this beautiful partnership, who we can refer families to and students to get counseling, and those kinds of things. 'Cause a lot of times I'm dealing with things . . . even with people coming to the homeschool program, there's some other stuff going. Sometimes it's not just academics.

C: So you can take care of the whole child, not just academics; it's also emotional.

A: *We have to.* Yes, because if you are emotionally out of it, what can you learn? If your parents are fighting at home and you're in the middle of that, you're not turning your homework in. So a lot of times parents don't understand your whole family is getting ready to be uncovered, but it's not bad. It's good. God loves you, there's some accountability that's coming, and you have the opportunity to make this better for real!

In Black home education, community plays a critical role in creating educational justice for our children's learning. Black home education communities embody values aligned with an African worldview known as Ubuntu. The African concept of Ubuntu, commonly translated as "I am because you/we are," contrasts sharply with American values of individualism and competition.[1] People who live by Ubuntu believe the only way they can know themselves is by being in community with others. Ubuntu tells us that through interdependence with others, we learn about ourselves.[2] Desmond Tutu explains, "A person with Ubuntu is open and available to others, affirming of others, does not feel threatened that others are able and good, for he or she has a proper self-assurance that comes from knowing that he or she belongs in a greater whole and is diminished when others are humiliated or diminished, when others are tortured or oppressed."[3] Ubuntu does not value competition with others, or the concept of survival of the fittest. Through Ubuntu, we can learn to see that regardless of our differences, as human beings we are interconnected. That interconnectedness has tremendous meaning to each person and the community.

The foregoing interview excerpt serves as an exemplar of Ubuntu found among Black home educators in my research. Alana, who homeschooled her three children and serves as a homeschool leader in her community for two different groups, exhibits Ubuntu in her approach to leadership. As a homeschool leader, Alana is committed to meeting each family where they are and ensuring that their needs are met, even if she cannot meet those needs herself. Alana includes the needs of parents as well as students in her Ubuntu-like leadership approach, and she focuses on the needs of family units. Notice Alana says "we have to" provide this level of care and support to members of the group. Though there are exceptions, most of the Black home educators I have met reflect this depth of commitment to one another. Alana's commitment to the families in her homeschool community aligns well with Ubuntu. She affirms her group members and helps them reach their goals and needs beyond academics. Members of the groups she directs will soon learn that being vulnerable within the group leads to edification and restoration. It is an authentically safe community. Alana serves culturally, linguistically, and racially diverse families in her homeschool groups and digitally across the country. Her Ubuntu-like leadership style represents her life view and perspective of community.

On the surface, home education would seem to align with neoliberal ideals of individualism and competition, which appear to govern all aspects of American life today.[4] Yet, as seen with Alana's example, Black home education is not always individualistic. Blurring the definitions of home education with self-directed learning, Renee Tougas reviewed the existing literature and found that Black home educators' perspectives and practices can "resist neoliberal entanglement when it is rooted in conceptions of self as part of the whole and where the development of autonomy is aimed at transforming sociopolitical and economic realities. This kind of SDE [self-directed education] creates an authentic disruption to neoliberal subjectivity."[5] Tougas further concludes that Black home educators' communal values, coupled with a critical examination, could result in pedagogies that resist neoliberalism. Thus, Black homeschool families' sense of community and Ubuntu-like values could inform teaching and learning practices in any setting, if educators have the courage and desire to resist neoliberalism's influence in today's teaching and learning practices.

Indeed, historically, we know that Ubuntu-like qualities existed among segregated Black communities. When school boards denied Black communities land or lumber to build their schools, community members who did not have children donated the necessary resources.[6] These Ubuntu-like actions were supported by cultural adages such as "Each one reach one," which served as a reminder to share with others and to bring others along as you advance. This chapter presents several ways contemporary Black home educators embody the spirit of this cultural adage.

Specifically, this chapter discusses the significance of the role of community in the lives of Black children and families who homeschool. The chapter documents deep relationships and connections Black home educators have built within their communities and beyond. The term *community* is broadly used throughout the chapter to refer to connections beyond geographic boundaries such as intergenerational relations. The concept of Ubuntu contributes to understanding the role of community in informing Black home educators' practices, ways of doing, and ways of knowing. Interestingly, none of my research studies have directly queried the role of community in Black home education. But this role is so intimately integrated in Black parents' homeschool practice that the topic emerged naturally as parents described their homeschool practice, which extended well beyond themselves.

UBUNTU-LIKE CHARACTERISTICS OF BLACK HOME EDUCATORS' SENSE OF COMMUNITY

Every Black home educator I have interviewed indicated that they knew at least one other Black homeschool mother who served as a guide or role model when they began homeschooling. This fact deeply connects to Ubuntu because Black mothers' home educator identities were typically formed within community among others rather than individually. Veteran home educators tended to refer to their early home education contacts as their mentors. These relationships began within homeschool groups and expanded beyond them. Even with these commonalities, Black homeschool mothers have established varying combinations of community support for themselves and for their children's learning.

To accommodate the varying characteristics of Black homeschool families' communities of support, rather than presenting findings thematically, I have provided exemplars of Black home educators' extended communities and the

Ubuntu-like characteristics within them. As predicted by Urie Bronfenbrenner's ecological systems theory, Black home educators' senses of community emerged from a broad context of entities extending beyond the home, such as churches, co-ops, local support groups, athletics, artistic or extracurricular pursuits, online homeschool groups, community-based organizations (e.g., YMCA, libraries, youth organizations), and neighbors in varying combinations.[7] The relationships and interactions within their diverse communities embodied Ubuntu-like characteristics such as respect for elders and veteran home educators, mutual trust, resource sharing, confidence building, encouragement, nurturing and mentoring, sustainability, vulnerability sharing, selflessness, and caring. The exemplars provided are intended to demonstrate how Black families experienced or demonstrated Ubuntu-like characteristics of community among their varying community sources.

Alana

This chapter opened with Alana's Ubuntu-like approach to serving as a leader of multiple homeschool organizations, but this was not her only form of community. Alana directs two homeschool organizations. One group is church based and the other is a homeschool program she described as follows:

> I also have another program, a learning center for homeschool families where we offer additional tutoring, and support for parents who may work and for single moms who may need just that extra. They know that their children need a smaller, more individualized kind of environment, but they need additional support beyond two days. I have about twenty families at that center. That's my own personal center. They usually come for two additional days from 9 until 2 p.m. Then they still have work that they must get done at home. But we actually hire moms, who are also Uber drivers, so they help with getting kids back and forth. Yeah, so it's really filling a need here.

Between the two programs, Alana sees herself and her team as supporting homeschool families, including families that usually would not be able to homeschool without the support the learning center is able to provide.

However, Alana's leadership style extends beyond creating opportunities for homeschool families to be supported academically. She shared,

> So one of the things that we believe is that we are part of the answer. We're on their [families'] team. Sometimes when parents are coming from especially a

> traditional environment to a homeschool environment, the parents don't realize how involved they are going to have to be. One of the things we've become really good at is [establishing] connections between the tutors and the parents. So if a student comes in, and they don't have their homework, then we're calling the parent, "Johnny doesn't have his homework." "Oh, we did it; it's in the bag." "Well, somehow it didn't make it to the classroom." So if that continues to happen, then we're calling the parents in for a conversation: "How can we help your child get what they need to get so they can get their work turned in and so their grades will be good?" Many times, what we begin to find out is what's really going on at home. And then when that gets opened up, we can say, "Why don't you try this?" or "You can try that." We may identify the problem that you and your husband are not on the same page. So what are some things that you can do? Because right now your child is playing you guys.

Alana further explained,

> We had to change our mind-set. I'm a homeschooler who homeschooled the old-fashioned way back in the eighties when homeschooling was just becoming legal. We've homeschooled for over twenty years. So when this new tribe came up with parents who are working and they're busy . . . at first I was like, I quit, because this is not homeschooling. One day I was really contemplating, "I can't do this, I can't do this." But God was saying to me there are no second-class citizens in homeschooling [Alana]. There are no second-class citizens; they are homeschoolers. They are doing it different from you. Their children are coming up in a different time from when your children came up because society is different. So figure that out because if most of these kids tried to get into another homeschooling group, they would be shunned. Because they don't meet up. You know, because they are not academically strong, because maybe they have some behavior issues in other locations. So if you don't take them, then what happens?

In contrast to the neoliberal approach to education, which appears to value a one-size-fits-all teaching style, Alana learned to embrace ways of homeschooling children that differed from her own approach, and she created a supportive space for those alternative approaches while also keeping the families' fundamental needs a priority. This translated to a change in how she viewed the children as well. She explained,

> I had to change my own heart. I had to stop seeing bad kids. I had to stop seeing troubles as a problem. Then I had to transmit that new way of thinking to my staff. So that when they came to me, "Bobby hit so-and-so," we need to call Bobby

> up to [remind him] who he really is and tell him, "That's not who you are. This is who you really are." And then give him assignments and things that show [that] what we say, he is. Okay, he is a leader. Then what can we do to give him something to lead here to begin to show him his true potential? The change took time to develop, but if the culture of the organization embraces the value that everyone matters, these are the types of changes necessary to live out that ideal.

Imagine if instead of referring students whom we see as having behavior problems to "the office," in-school suspension, or some other punitive response, we took the time to find out what was really causing the student to act out and worked on that problem. This is a reminder of the need for healing in our schools and communities. Yes, there are probably a lot of children who would need this type of support. Yes, it would take a lot of time and energy. Yes, this would require school districts or states to hire a lot more social workers, guidance counselors, and other professionals and experts, but it would also get to the heart of the issue. Could group counseling become part of the school day? Could states or school districts partner with higher education institutions to provide preprofessionals in the needed areas to engage in supervised practice to serve children in need? Maybe I am dreaming big here, but I believe considering partnerships such as these, which mimic what Alana does for the homeschool community she serves, would be better than just letting children fall through the cracks or become part of the school-to-prison pipeline just because it is easier for us as teachers and administrators, or because we do not know what else to do.

Alana, the mother of three children who were now adults, related her homeschool leadership approach to her motivations to homeschool. When explaining her motivation to homeschool, she shared,

> I don't want to offend anyone, but I'll tell you the truth. I was noticing this shift in [my children's] personality in a negative way when other people's children were getting on that bus to go to school. I noticed a shift in their faith, a shift in their attitude, and I noticed that as that continued to when they became teenagers, the parents were losing them. So I began to make the connection there's something about the school, or there's something about the parent at home, that's not strong enough to overcome what's going on at the school. And it was really important to us [Alana and her husband] for our children to have our faith. To believe what we believe. It was a kind of a fear that started us on the homeschool journey, to be quite honest.

Alana perceived a spiritual disconnection between home and school that had created what appeared to be a disruption to the family bond, which compelled her to teach her children at home. As a result, her work as a home education leader also aims to resolve challenges to family bonds. When families are first admitted in her learning center for home educators, she and her team take the time to help families first process their transition from traditional schools. This is an important first step that sometimes gets ignored. Often, when parents turn to home education, they are choosing a lifestyle that they themselves have never experienced. This takes courage.

Alana's homeschool practice began in the 1980s when homeschooling was not popular, especially among Black families. Even back then, she embodied Ubuntu-like practices that benefited more than her own family. She extended her home education in a way that benefited the children and families she lived near at the time. Alana shared,

> You know, for twenty-eight years we were in this totally Black low-income community and your kids are so different. But one of the things that we did, we didn't come out thinking our children were better than others. We had a ministry in the neighborhood, Bible club, we had church. The neighborhood kids were coming into our house. We changed our basement into a learning center, and we tutored. So that's the model for our kids. People are people. But we connect, we allowed them [Alana's children] to connect with the community in ways that would be positive, through education and the Word and those kinds of things.

With her children now in their thirties, Alana's homeschool leadership represented coming full circle, in a sense, because what she did for her family and her neighborhood community, she now trained others to do. Alana's example demonstrates the selflessness of an Ubuntu-like community and went beyond providing simple encouragement. The culture of the community she established engaged in resolving deep-seated issues within families.

Toni

Toni, a home educator of her two youngest children, learned about home education from a friend who homeschooled but lived far away from her. Toni shared, "I had a good friend that homeschools her children, but she lived in a very rural town, so she didn't have access to any support group. To be honest, there was a support group in her area that was established, it was just a little bit away from her. But she experienced little prejudices within that group and so she just went on her own. Then she started sharing with me about the benefits of it and so I just thought, you know, I could try." Previously, Toni's children had attended a private Christian school. But she found the learning environment too restrictive for young children, as she described: "You know, be quiet and stand in the hall, in the line, don't move, hands to your side, and then [her daughter] wouldn't let me sit down [at home]!" Her daughter was four years old at the time. Her friend's home education experiences made the approach seem worth trying to Toni because it would provide a more nurturing learning environment for her children.

Describing her initial homeschool practice, Toni shared, "And once I tried, I just, you know, at that time, we were in the lower grades. So we did something called unit studies where you just take a certain subject, and you do all your work around that subject. You do language arts, math, and all of that. And so that's how I was exposed to it." She used integrated thematic units with support from her friend to begin her home education practice. Thematic units at this young age might include a weeklong focus on a color. Let's say this week's theme is blue. The children will read about things that are blue, they will do art projects in different shades of blue, they will have blue snacks, they will be encouraged to wear blue each day, and so forth. Blue becomes the focal point of all subject areas (reading, math, art, music, etc.). The idea is that by immersing the children in a variety of experiences with different forms of blue, they will develop a strong understanding of blue. Imagine an integrated unit on apples or the Civil War for older children.

Toni's homeschool community began to grow. She shared, "Then I heard of another group here in the [metropolitan area]. So that made it even more beneficial for me. There were veterans out there that had graduated kids and they've gone on to be engineers and so forth. So I was like, 'Okay, I can do it too!' [*Laughs.*]" This group was so beneficial that her friend who was homeschooling in a rural area moved to the metropolitan area near Toni and joined the support group as well. As Toni's daughters grew, her homeschool community continued to grow as well. The girls participated in a speech club to develop their public speaking skills. Toni also shared, "We just joined a crochet—like we used to call it years ago, social circle clubs. But this lady, she is an African American Martha Stewart! You know? We're part of a group of with various ages in the group learning how to knit, how to hook, how to crochet. My oldest daughter is in a math club, they also do dance, and it would be easier to say what I won't do because we end up being away from the house all the time!"

Having a friend who found homeschooling beneficial prompted Toni to begin homeschooling because the traditional school environment did not align with what Toni desired for her children's learning experience. Once she began her homeschool practice, she continued to research other community resources and found sustainability through a local group. Engagement with veteran home educators and their families played an important role in keeping Toni motivated and building her confidence as a home educator. The large urban area had so many community resources to support her homeschool practice that her friend from the rural area actually moved there too.

Talisha

Talisha is a veteran home educator of seven children, whom she and her husband home educated from birth. She had been homeschooling for fifteen years at the time of our interview. Recounting the initial years of her home education practice, Talisha shared, "We were part of a homeschooling network where the older, mature homeschooling mamas and dads would encourage us. So likewise, I have been a mentor in my group for several years now. But also, a lot of times, the people I end up mentoring are people not from the group. Just people I meet at church that are new to homeschooling." Here Talisha demonstrates the reciprocity of Black home education's Ubuntu-like mentoring and nurturing, and how her mentoring of home educators extended outside her homeschool co-op.

Although Talisha's background was not in education, her home educator identity enabled her to bond with public school teachers in multiple settings. For example, when describing the criticism that she endured from her family for choosing to home educate her children, Talisha shared,

> I have a neighbor across the street. She taught in the New York public schools for her whole career, and I've known her now . . . since we moved into this house. She is like a mom to me. [*Talking to one of her children, she says, "Who am I talking about? Who's my mom?" Child replies . . . , "Mrs. XXX."*] She is such a godsend. So even when my mother discouraged me in homeschooling, Mrs. XXX encouraged me. She knows the time that you spend with the kids is fleeting. Really, I mean, if you think about it, it's really only eighteen to twenty years.

Talisha's teacher community of support also included a mother she met while serving in her church. She reported, "I was working at the [church program] two days a week, and one of the moms that was involved was a [historically Black college and university graduate] and a teacher. She still is a teacher, but she has called me on occasion to inquire, 'How do I homeschool my son, because the system is failing him?' This is a teacher! But she taught at the [church program] like I did, and she was a good teacher, so I felt comfortable with [my daughter] being in her setting two days a week in the [church program]."

Talisha found camaraderie as a home educator with people in and outside her homeschool co-op group. Like Toni, she appreciated the presence of veteran home educators who nurtured her as she developed her homeschool practice. In turn, Talisha also found herself mentoring others as they turned to her for advice. Her identity as a home educator had been deeply developed within her community and extended beyond the community. Talisha's example also demonstrates the selflessness of Black home education. She did not keep all she had garnered from being mentored to herself. Instead, she gladly shared it with others, even those outside her homeschool community.

Moesha

Moesha actively used the word *community* to refer to the family home, and their responsibilities within the home, as part of her homeschool practice. She explained, "Our homework is our community work. I also call keeping our house clean 'community work.' Therefore, after schooling comes chores. So that's when we're washing clothes, vacuuming, sweeping, mopping. And then on certain days, we'll go and do outside community work."

Later in our interview, Moesha revealed how her homeschool practice expanded the definition of community. Her children participated in chess club on Wednesdays, art club on another day, and so forth. She explained where those activities took place: "They are done through our support group at different locations. For example, our art class—our teacher teaches at [a local library]. They have a room in the library. Our chess club is at one of our support group member's church family life center. Then there's another church where we meet on Friday for our presentation day for the smaller children, third grade and under. Our advanced fifth grade and up have speech club that day. So all of the children are learning how to present orally." This homeschool group pieced together gathering places for their children's extracurricular activities by sharing members' resources and local community resources. So, as Black communities did during Reconstruction when they were denied land, lumber, or transportation to build their children's schools, the community chipped in to ensure there were places and access to education for Black children.

Furthermore, Moesha described social activities that her local homeschool community group planned. She explained,

> We have what we call unstructured activity days for our group outside of just fun park days. And that begins in October. So we have six months the fourth Friday of the month where we'll go bowling twice, we'll go skating twice, and we'll go to the park twice. And so therefore when *all* of us come together, that's when the community or the majority of the people can see, "All y'all homeschool?" We didn't realize how many kids we had until we got to the park. The last time we went to the park in April—we had at least thirty to forty families, and we have a few families that just have one child; the average family had three or four children. So it's over a hundred children at any given time when we get together for park day.

This homeschool group was parent led, and with so many families to serve, they had to plan and schedule events, as well as share resources to identify locations to serve the group. The large number of activities and events demonstrates the active participation among the families.

When parents got together in person or online, they readily shared resources, and when one person found an effective tutor or program, the word spread among the group quickly. Moesha shared,

> With church, with the group, and even with our outside school activities, we have . . . People say, "Well, how are you going to handle chemistry? How're you going to handle biology?" We have educated individuals that have master's [degrees] and stuff who are teaching these classes in their homes. So when we get to high-school-level science, we have [a group member] who has a master's and a doctorate in chemistry who has a biology setting in her house that she uses to teach ninth-through-twelfth-grade science for us. We have someone that has a master's in literature—if I want British lit—and I have a French tutor. I have—we have the skills in our group, and we pull from that group. So therefore, after our own individual schooling hours, we set aside time in that class. "Okay, who needs a French tutor?" We had an email out—someone needed a

> Chinese tutor. I was like, "Man, we're teaching Chinese." The same goes for other needs . . . so whatever needs come up in our village, the group is for each other. "Okay, I need a printer. Does anybody have a printer?" "I need a file cabinet." . . . As our children get older, "Okay, somebody can use these clothes." "Okay, he outgrew these. These are still good. Who has a boy that needs a size so-and-so?"—that's what our support group is like for us—"Come and pick 'em up." Or "We're finished with this grade. Who needs this grade work?" You know? We're all tending to help wherever the need is. So that is a family.

In this example, Moesha goes back and forth between saying "I have" and "we have" as she describes this aspect of resource sharing. Both are true. This is another demonstration of the Ubuntu-like climate of Black homeschool groups. We all have because I have. In this way, home educators are not alone in their homeschool practice and in attempting to meet the unique needs of their children. This is a critical feature of the homeschool community because many Black homeschool families must sacrifice one parent's income, which reduces their financial status.[8]

Monica

Monica, a married mother of five who also homeschooled her children from birth, described the pivotal role homeschool group memberships served in informing her home education practice and the significance of Ubuntu-like values among the homeschool group.

Homeschool groups serve as a conduit for information for home educators. Monica participated in several types of groups. She was an active member of online groups that had newsletters with information on curriculum, community events, and children/youth programs particularly designed for homeschool families. Throughout our interview, as she shared about various community-based activities and programs her children participated in, I would ask how she learned about them and her response would be, "From the newsletters and emails posted by one of the groups I belong to." Monica was also an active member of a local co-op, where her children took courses in subject areas, the arts, and enrichment. The co-op was housed in a church, but it functioned independently of the church. The co-op offered courses from kindergarten through twelfth grade. Certified teachers provided specialized courses in some areas such as the sciences for the co-op, but homeschool parents taught most of the classes offered there. This parent-led co-op expected parents to contribute in some way.

Monica was also an active member of a local predominantly Black homeschool support group in her community. Describing how much she valued this local community group, she shared,

> But what's been nice is that I think that homeschoolers need support, and this group has over forty families and there's just a lot of support. Last year I was the new members coordinator, and I would get a lot of calls from people who were just starting to home school and they're really scared and they hope they're doing what's right for their kids and all this. I've been a part of several meetings where people have addressed people's fears and talked about how, "Yeah, I fear too," and "I've been there."

Here Monica demonstrates the close-knit, safe space created by this local homeschool community group. Parents had a space where they could share their vulnerabilities as home educators, and they experienced mutual trust. As a result, the co-op served as a place where their courage to homeschool could be reinforced so they could continue. The veteran home educators in the group helped establish meaningful relationships among the families. Monica explained, "We have people in our group who have kids now in college, [and at] a little panel discussion for other kids who were in college, they came back and talked to the other kids about their experience, and whether they felt like they were prepared, after having been homeschooled through high school and all of that. I think that was actually good not just for kids but for the parents, you know, like, 'Look, I can actually homeschool my child and get them into college.'" Here the homeschool support group appears to contribute to parents' self-image and to sustain parents' beliefs in the possibilities and opportunities created by choosing to homeschool.

The local community group Monica and her family participated in created community for the children as well. She explained,

> I think the concept is it is important to have things, activities for the kids to do with each other so the kids don't feel isolated and don't feel like, "I don't have any friends." We, my husband and I, run a teen activity group. So once a month we have teens do things together, and that's really important when they get to be teenagers; that's when they're really looking for socialization. We've been able to have them speak to other teens around them and sometimes through that they connect, and they'll email and chat with each other, in between the times that we get together. And so that is very important, I think. There's always the need for that support and part of the group. Then you find out about these different classes that you can take and different people teaching classes and getting people

> together just to work on a curriculum, as a group. During the summertime, our subdivision has a pool, so there'll be a number of people. . . . The pool is never used during the daytime, so the parents who work, they still have to have the kids go somewhere else, so I'll have a group come over and just hang out at the pool. So once again the kids just getting together. The idea that the kids feel like they have—they're part of a community and this idea that the parents feel like they can get the support and the encouragement, specifically the encouragement that they need to continue homeschooling, because, you know, you're doing something different and because you feel like you may be failing them.

These efforts to care for, mentor, and nurture one another within the community provided authentic uplift and support to help Black home educators sustain their practice. Monica's willingness to support working home educators by providing a place for their children to go in the summertime is of note. This extension of care would also tremendously support single-parent homeschool households.

These few excerpts from the research reveal the presence of Ubuntu-like values among Black homeschool groups. Such groups value insight gained from the veteran or elder home educators in the group and intentionally keep them engaged in the homeschool community. Although all of Monica's children had long since graduated from college, she remained an active member of the homeschool community and most recently had cofounded a statewide Black homeschool organization. Veteran Black home educators continue to serve as mentors and guides even when their own children become adults.

Mutual trust permeated this group and continues to do so. Home educators are not in competition with one another. Instead, they embody the "Each one reach one" adage. Some of the Black homeschool groups obtain a high level of intimacy through the authentic and selfless care extended among group members. They remain vulnerable with one another by sharing their challenges, which leads to collaboration in their problem-solving. To reach this point, Black homeschool group members demonstrate they have a vested interest beyond their own self-interests and needs.

CHALLENGES ACCESSING DISTRICT RESOURCES IN THE COMMUNITY

Many Black home educators identified accessing resources from their local school district to support their children's learning as one of their greatest challenges to home education. Parents were driven to seek resources for situations such as addressing their children's learning challenges, assessing possible learning disabilities, participating in enrichment activities, or even playing on school athletic teams.

Moesha, a home educator of four children, described the challenge of seeking support from her local school district to help address her son's speech development. She shared,

> Other than our other homeschoolers, you will rarely get outside support. And what I mean by that is my son, my third grader, his speech is a little slow. So he takes a speech class. He does speech development. We have tried for many years to get help from [the county school district] to provide a speech class for him. The help that we got from them by the time he was four was he went to [a local school] for their special education program. He went through [a private diagnostic health-care organization]. They tested him and they said, "Oh, this should be the class that can help him. He can get speech and he can get a lot of other help." Well, he started that class in October. He got on the school bus and went to [the local school].
>
> In the beginning, the [speech] teacher had about four students and they had a new [classroom] teacher. She was totally motivated in helping the children. She was surprised at how much [my son] already knew. He would be sent off to the speech teacher for help. Well, by the end of that year—he went from October to May—that class of four had grown to a class of eleven. No longer was it a special ed class. Well maybe that's what they considered special ed, but to me it was more of a behavioral control class. The children added to the class behavior problems—so much so that one of the children in this class needed special attention. He took up most of her time, most of her attention. We learned that the teacher was overwhelmed with how many students that she had. All [my son] did in her speech class was cry. She'd have to bring in another student that he felt comfortable with not to cry, but she could no longer get him to speak. So I'm saying, "But no one told me this."
>
> So now this is May. I'm coming in for the conference and I'm talking with each of the individual teachers and I'm like, "Well, Ms. So-and-So, why didn't you tell me this?" Well, that was the classroom teacher, and he wasn't having any problems in the class. This was the speech teacher. And the speech teacher never told the class teacher, so therefore nothing was written home to me. I had brought my other children with [my son] to the conference, and they sat in the back while we were talking. The speech teacher watched him communicate with his siblings. She said, "This is the most I've ever heard [your son] speak." He was there all day, which was from 8:00 to 12:15! So that was a waste. I had still done most of the teaching at home—still in that sense—because he didn't gain anything from that

> experience. We had to go through the insurance company to get him speech elsewhere.

Similarly, Toni, who lived in a different district but the same state as Moesha, shared,

> I had a difficult situation with the little one. Her language wasn't progressing as I thought it should. So I contacted our school district, because you have to turn in your attendance sheets every month, and so I reached out to the homeschool liaison with the public school to see if [my daughter] could have access to a speech therapist. But she really gave me a hard time. I had to remind her I am still a taxpaying citizen. You know, there's a vacant desk . . . you still have my books, you have all those—you know, everything you need as if my child was there. You know, not to, then she did what she needed to do to let me have access to the speech support. She was counting it as something as extracurricular and I wasn't trying to get involved in sports or anything, I was just trying to see if I had that option, and I did. But I was trying to go through her, so sometimes, they're a little prejudiced. You know, if our kids are doing well, whatever, they don't get the credit.

In each of these examples, Black home educators sought support for their children's learning challenges from their local school district. In Moesha's example, when the support provided by the school district required her to enroll her son in a public school–based program, the family experienced many of the challenges experienced by Black families in traditional schools, including a lack of communication, which led to disenfranchisement of parental engagement in the child's education. Had the teacher notified Moesha of the challenges and subsequent setbacks to her son's learning, then Moesha would have had the opportunity to intervene and seek a better setting for her child instead of having to wait until the end of the school year to learn about it.

In Toni's example, she asked the school district's homeschool contact person how to access support services for her child's speech development challenges. When the contact person attempted to deny Toni's child access to those services, Toni became frustrated and had to push for what she knew her child was entitled to according to state laws. While Toni's child did get served as needed, the school district contact's initial denial demonstrates either a lack of knowledge of the laws or, as Toni speculated, the contact's resentment of home education families.

The next section shares examples of what can happen when local school districts, and state laws, consider the needs of homeschool families and their children—in other words, how local school districts and states can become more Ubuntu-like in their approach to partnering with homeschool families.

SCHOOL DISTRICT–HOME EDUCATION PARTNERSHIPS

Not all school districts shun homeschooled children's access to public school resources. In recent years, local school districts have increasingly created avenues for homeschool families to access district resources.[9] For example, Iowa homeschool legislation enables homeschool students to enroll in homeschooling and public education simultaneously.[10] This open-enrollment law provides home education students with freedom to choose public school courses while also learning at home and gives them access to athletics and other forms of extracurricular activities. Iowa's home education law also gives local school districts the freedom to offer assistance programs to homeschool families.[11] These programs provide homeschool students access to textbooks and standardized testing, as well as the ability to confer with a certified teacher. Local schools receive state funds based on a partial count of .1 student for each homeschool student who enrolls in Iowa's dual enrollment program and .3 student for each student who enrolls in Iowa's homeschool assistance program, which makes these programs mutually beneficial.

Similar programs have been developed to address the unique nature of home education families' needs and state resources. Alaska serves as an example of what can happen within an effective partnership with homeschool families. According to one study, "Alaska's unique geography has driven it to develop a novel system for supporting homeschool families through correspondence programs. In Alaska, funding for homeschooling is provided directly to individual families through district-run correspondence programs. If a family choose to enroll in an accredited home learning program, they may use an annual per-pupil allotment to purchase textbooks and other educational resources."[12] Efforts to overcome the geographic challenge of educating children in Alaska have led to a viable solution for the state's homeschool families.

Partnering with homeschool families is not a new idea for local school districts or states. In 1999, the Association for Supervision and Curriculum Development published an article on this topic stating,

> How can we effectively integrate home-schooled students into schools, districts, and programs? What can individual schools do to help home-schooled students

> make the transition into the public school classroom? And what can students learn from one another? Any program that attempts to integrate a new population of students into the existing one raises similar issues. We asked the same kind of questions when we chose to mainstream disabled students. We ask them when we integrate various cultures into the classroom. The first step, as always, begins with awareness.[13]

Research on Black home education has certainly created such an awareness, for those who read it. But the author of this article did not have the benefit of that research. Focusing on the challenge of her time, she wrote,

> Another reason for homeschooling is dissatisfaction with the public-school curriculum. For example, parents of gifted or disabled students are sometimes displeased with the quality of education that their children receive in public school and may choose to work with them one-on-one instead. These parents are more likely to return to the schools if they find opportunities that fulfill their children's needs. . . . What you may notice is that these parents all take an active interest in their child's education. Ironically, these are the kinds of parents we wish we had more of in schools.[14]

Hopefully, schools do value actively engaged parents from all backgrounds. If so, there are numerous opportunities to intentionally partner with home educators from all backgrounds in mutually beneficial ways. This dated article provides several suggestions. The author ends it with a charge for school personnel: "It is in every school's best interest to serve any and all of its students."[15] Twenty-five years later, this charge remains true.

Funding serves as one of the major points of conflict in school district–home education partnerships. States have started passing laws to create education savings accounts (ESAs) that provide financial support for homeschooling as well as other forms of alternative education.[16] ESA laws vary slightly state to state, but typically they enable parents to purchase materials directly related to instruction. However, ESA laws have stirred controversy. While the support provided by the laws can assist a financially challenged family in acquiring curriculum materials and addressing other learning needs so that they can more effectively homeschool, the funds may require some sort of oversight from the state, which most home education families want to avoid. Additionally, there is concern about the use of state funds acquired through taxpayer money to support non-state-funded learning options such as home education or private school education. But as Toni stated, home educators are also taxpayers. Shouldn't their children also have a right to access state support for their education?

My research demonstrates that if the schools provided a learning setting that addressed their children's needs and ensured their safety, many Black home educators would have kept their children enrolled in their locally assigned public schools (see chapter 1). States typically have laws that promise a "basic" education. In Georgia, for example, the Quality Basic Education Act of 1986 states, "The purpose of the Act is to provide 'quality basic education.'" The law further states that it is "designed to give students equal access to educational resources regardless of the wealth of their county of residence."[17] As I have written about elsewhere, many of the Black parents who participated in my research did not find this equal access to be the reality—they had been assigned to local schools located in deeply underresourced portions of their school districts. The schools had become resegregated, predominantly Black or Brown, and overcrowded.[18] Most Black parents want their public schools to work for their children, but they often do not. In many ways, racialized experiences, and the inequity within urban schools and between urban and suburban and rural schools, have led Black parents to home educate. Decades of leadership have not been able to resolve these issues, and therefore Black families increasingly choose home education to create their own educational justice for their children. But doesn't the state still need to do its part on behalf of all children, even homeschooled students, to ensure a sound basic education as promised in state law?

CONCLUSION

Overall, what we learn from Black home educators reminds us to prioritize children's interests and needs, to remain flexible, and to consider the needs of others instead of just ourselves when developing policy and practice related to education. Policy and practice that serve children first would focus on ensuring racial and cultural affirmation and representation of all students. In addition, educators would be held accountable for being culturally competent and culturally relevant in their instructional practices. This is the opposite of what is occurring in the US today. The goals of diversity, equity, and inclusion have been removed from standards and policy by law in numerous states. All students need critical thinking skills and teachers' high expectations. Black home educators promote their children's independence, which encourages students to own their responsibility for their education. Rather than trying to control children's bodies, we could be exploring ways to insert more voice and choice into their learning experiences. Instead of employing zero-tolerance policies, teaching to the test, and creating school-to-prison pipelines, we could be focused on wellness, well-being, and the humanity of teaching and learning.

Black home educators' experiences reveal the lingering painful practices that have never worked. These educators have had the courage to resist present circumstances, and they have set out to create their own educational justice; not just for themselves but for each other as well. Imagine if those developing educational policy and practice in the US could have the same courage to do what is necessary and right on behalf of all children, one classroom, one school, or one school district at a time.

Notes

Introduction

1. Kerry McDonald, "Not-Back-to-School Time for Homeschoolers: As Support Systems Strengthen, More Families Embrace New Approach to Education," The 74, September 21, 2023, https://www.the74million.org/article/not-back-to-school-time-for-homeschoolers-as-support-systems-strengthen-more-families-embrace-new-approach-to-education/.
2. Brian Ray, "On Blacks Choosing Home-Based Education," National Home Education Research Institute, October 10, 2007, https://www.nheri.org/home-school-researcher-on-blacks-choosing-home-based-education/.
3. Cheryl Fields-Smith and Meca Williams, "Motivations, Sacrifices, and Challenges: Black Parents' Decisions to Home School," *Urban Review* 41, no. 4 (2009): 369–89.
4. Cheryl Fields-Smith, *Exploring Single Black Mothers' Resistance Through Homeschooling* (New York: Palgrave Macmillan, 2020); Cheryl Fields-Smith, "From Our Ancestors to Today: The Significance of Contemporary Black Homeschooling in the U.S.," in *Homeschooling Black Children in the U.S.: Theory, Practice, and Popular Culture*, ed. Khadijah Z. Ali-Coleman and Cheryl Fields-Smith (Charlotte, NC: Information Age, 2022), 1–15.
5. Meca Williams-Johnson and Cheryl Fields-Smith, "Homeschooling Among Black Families as a Form of Parental Involvement: A Focus on Parental Role Construction, Efficacy, and Emotions," *Educational Psychologist* 57, no. 4 (2022): 252–66.
6. Fields-Smith, *Single Black Mothers' Resistance*, 139–42.
7. Kevin Welner and Prudence L. Carter, "Achievement Gaps Arise from Opportunity Gaps," in *Closing the Opportunity Gap: What America Must Do to Give Every Child an Even Chance*, ed. Prudence L. Carter and Kevin Welner (New York: Oxford University Press, 2013), 1–10.
8. See, for example, Fabienne Doucet, "Parent Involvement as Ritualized Practice," *Anthropology & Education Quarterly* 42, no. 4 (2011): 404–21; Latisha L. Ross, Aixa D. Marchand, Vaness O. Cox, and Stephanie J. Rowley, "Racial Identity as a Context for African American Parents' School Trust and Involvement and the Impact on Student Preparation and Persistence," *Contemporary Educational Psychology* 55 (2018): 1–11; Denise Yull, Lisa V. Blitz, Tonia Thompson, and Carla Murray, "Can We Talk? Using Community-Based Participatory Action Research to Build Family and School Partnerships with Families of Color," *School Community Journal* 24, no. 2 (2014): 9–31.
9. Brian Ray, "A Systematic Review of the Empirical Research on Selected Aspects of Homeschooling as a School Choice," *Journal of School Choice* 11, no. 4 (2017): 604–21.
10. Brian Ray, "African American Homeschool Parents' Motivations for Homeschooling and Their Black Children's Academic Achievement," *Journal of School Choice* 9, no. 1 (2015): 71–96.
11. Cheryl Fields-Smith and Meca Williams, "Motivations, Sacrifices, and Challenges: Black Parents' Decisions to Home School," *Urban Review* 41, no. 4 (2009): 369–89.
12. Kathleen V. Hoover-Dempsey and Howard M. Sandler, "Why Do Parents Become Involved in Their Children's Education?," *Review of Educational Research* 67, no. 1 (1997): 3–42;

Jane A. Van Galen, "Ideology, Curriculum, and Pedagogy in Home Education," *Urban Education* 21, no. 1 (1988): 52–68.

13. Fields-Smith and Williams, "Motivations, Sacrifices, and Challenges."
14. Fields-Smith and Williams, 377.
15. Williams-Johnson and Fields-Smith, "Homeschooling Among Black Families."
16. Ama Mazama and Garvey Lundy, "African American Homeschooling as Racial Protectionism," *Journal of Black Studies* 43, no. 7 (2012): 723–48; Cheryl Fields-Smith and Monica Wells Kisura, "Resisting the Status Quo: The Narratives of Black Homeschoolers in Metro-Atlanta and Metro-DC," *Peabody Journal of Education* 88, no. 3 (2013): 265–83.
17. bell hooks, "Homeplace (a Site of Resistance)," in *Yearning: Race, Gender, and Cultural Politics* (Boston: South End, 1990), 41–49.
18. Fields-Smith and Wells Kisura, "Resisting the Status Quo," 266.
19. Fields-Smith and Wells Kisura, 267.
20. Cynthia B. Dillard, *On Spiritual Strivings: Transforming an African American Woman's Academic Life* (New York: State University of New York Press, 2006).
21. Alex Zamalin, *Struggle on Their Minds: The Political Thought of African American Resistance* (New York: Columbia University Press, 2017).
22. Zamalin.
23. Combahee River Collective, "The Combahee River Collective Statement," 1977, http://circuitous.org/scraps/combahee.html.
24. Patricia Hill Collins, *Black Feminist Thought: Knowledge, Consciousness, and the Politics of Empowerment* (London: Routledge, 2008).
25. Dillard, *On Spiritual Strivings*.
26. Dillard.
27. Najarian R. Peters, "The Right to Be and Become: Black Home-Educators as Child Privacy Protectors," *Michigan Journal of Race and Law* 25, no. 1 (2020): 21–59.
28. Peters, 26.
29. Peters, 30 (emphasis in the original).
30. Peters.
31. Vanessa Siddle Walker, *Their Highest Potential: An African American School Community in the Segregated South* (Chapel Hill: University of North Carolina Press, 1996).
32. Walker, 271.
33. Jarvis R. Givens, *Fugitive Pedagogy: Carter G. Woodson and the Art of Black Teaching* (Cambridge, MA: Harvard University Press, 2021).
34. Michael J. Dumas, "'Losing an Arm': Schooling as a Site of Black Suffering," *Race Ethnicity and Education* 17, no. 1 (2014): 1–29; Bettina L. Love, *We Want to Do More Than Survive: Abolitionist Teaching and the Pursuit of Educational Freedom* (Boston: Beacon, 2020).
35. Dumas, "'Losing an Arm'"; Love, *We Want to Do More*.
36. Laura S. Abrams and Jewelle Taylor Gibbs, "Disrupting the Logic of Home-School Relations: Parent Involvement Strategies and Practices of Inclusion and Exclusion," *Urban Education* 37, no. 3 (2002): 384–407; Aixa D. Marchand et al., "Integrating Race, Racism, and Critical Consciousness in Black Parents' Engagement with Schools," *Journal of Family Theory and Review* 11, no. 3 (2019): 341–487; Camille Wilson Cooper, "Parent Involvement, African American Mothers, and the Politics of Educational Care," *Equity and Excellence in Education* 42, no. 4 (2009): 379–94.

Chapter 1

1. Darlene F. Williams, "Estimated Median Incomes for FY 2006," US Department of Housing and Urban Development, March 8, 2006, https://www.huduser.gov/portal/datasets/il/il06/MedianNotice_2006.pdf.
2. For a detailed discussion of the sacrifices made by Black homeschool families in this study, see Cheryl Fields-Smith and Meca Williams, "Motivations, Sacrifices, and Challenges: Black Parents' Decisions to Homeschool," *Urban Review* 41, no. 4 (2009): 369–89.
3. For a detailed description of this comparative study, see Cheryl Fields-Smith and Monica Wells Kisura, "Resisting the Status Quo: The Narratives of Black Homeschoolers in Metro-Atlanta and Metro-DC," *Peabody Journal of Education* 88, no. 3 (2013): 267.
4. Irving Seidman, *Interviewing as Qualitative Research: A Guide for Researchers in Education and Social Sciences*, 3rd ed. (New York: Teachers College Press, 2005).
5. Christina M. Greer, *Black Ethnics: Race, Immigration, and the Pursuit of the American Dream* (Oxford: Oxford University Press, 2013).
6. Jane A. Van Galen, "Ideologues and Pedagogues: Parents Who Teach Their Children at Home," in *Home Schooling: Political, Historical, and Pedagogical Perspectives*, ed. Jane Van Galen and Mary Anne Pitman (Norwood, NJ: Ablex, 1991), 63–76.
7. Cheryl Fields-Smith, *Exploring Single Black Mothers' Resistance Through Homeschooling* (New York: Palgrave Macmillan, 2020); Fields-Smith and Kisura, "Resisting the Status Quo."
8. Van Galen, "Ideologues and Pedagogues."
9. Fields-Smith, *Single Black Mothers' Resistance*, 61–82.
10. Beth Hatt, "Smartness as a Cultural Practice in Schools," *American Educational Research Journal* 49, no. 3 (2012): 438–60.
11. Karl Aubrey and Alison Riley, *Understanding and Using Educational Theories* (Los Angeles: Sage, 2016).
12. Diane Ravitch, *The Death and Life of the Great American School System: How Testing and Choice Are Undermining Education* (New York: Basic Books, 2010).
13. Kathleen V. Hoover-Dempsey and Howard M. Sandler, "Why Do Parents Become Involved in Their Children's Education?," *Review of Educational Research* 67, no. 1 (1997): 3–42.
14. Akilah S. Richards, *Raising Free People: Unschooling as Liberation and Healing Work* (Oakland, CA: PM Press, 2020).
15. Anneliese A. Singh, *The Racial Healing Handbook: Practical Activities to Help You Challenge Privilege, Confront Systemic Racism, and Engage in Collective Healing* (Oakland, CA: New Harbinger, 2019), 33–43.
16. Richard Kluger, *Simple Justice: The History of* Brown v. Board of Education *and Black America's Struggle for Equality* (New York: Vintage Books).

Chapter 2

1. Kris Manjapra, "Resistance Is Healing," Global Histories of Resistance, https://www.historiesofresistance.com/resistance-as-healing.
2. Shaneé A. Washington et al., "'It's a Vibe': Belonging, Healing, and Liberation in Community Spaces by Us and for Us," *Equity and Excellence in Education*, published ahead of print, October 8, 2023, 3, https://doi.org/10.1080/10665684.2023.2262477.
3. Latoya Sherrica Johnson, "Using Sista Circles to Examine the Professional Experience of Contemporary Black Women Teachers in Schools: A Collective Story About School Culture and Support" (PhD diss., University of Georgia, 2015); Neal-Barnett et al., "In the

Company of My Sisters: Sister Circles as an Anxiety Intervention for Professional African American Women," *Journal of Affective Disorders* 129 (2011): 213–18.

4. Anneliese A. Singh, *The Racial Healing Handbook: Practical Activities to Help You Challenge Privilege, Confront Systemic Racism, and Engage in Collective Healing* (Oakland, CA: New Harbinger, 2019), 32.
5. Amber M. Neal-Stanley, "'Out of the Mouths of Babes': Testimonies of Black Student Experiences in a Modern-Day Segregation Academy," *Religion and Education* 50, no. 4 (2023): 13.
6. Neal-Stanley, 14.
7. Neal-Stanley, 17.
8. Elizabeth Bartholet, "Homeschooling: Parent Rights Absolutism vs. Child Rights to Education & Protection," *Arizona Law Review* 62, no.1 (2020): 1–80.
9. Karen T. Craddock, ed., *Black Motherhood(s): Contours, Contexts and Considerations* (Bradford, ON: Demeter, 2015); Dawn Marie Dow, *Mothering While Black: Boundaries and Burdens of Middle-Class Parenthood* (Oakland: University of California Press, 2019).
10. Dani McClain, "What All Parents Can Learn from Black Mothers," *The Nation*, April 15, 2019, 15.
11. Akilah S. Richards, *Raising Free People: Unschooling as Liberation and Healing Work* (Oakland, CA: PM Press, 2020).
12. Cheryl Fields-Smith, *Exploring Single Black Mothers' Resistance Through Homeschooling* (New York: Palgrave Macmillan, 2020), 105–26.
13. Najarian R. Peters, "The Right to Be and Become: Black Home-Educators as Child Privacy Protectors," *Michigan Journal of Race and Law* 25, no. 1 (2019): 21–59.
14. Beverly Daniel Tatum, *Why Are All the Black Kids Sitting Together in the Cafeteria? And Other Conversations About Race* (New York: Basic Books, 2003).
15. Tatum.
16. Joy Harden Bradford, *Sisterhood Heals: The Transformative Power of Healing in Community* (New York: Ballantine Books, 2023), 22–23.
17. Cynthia B. Dillard, *On Spiritual Strivings: Transforming an African American Woman's Academic Life* (New York: State University of New York Press, 2006), 22.
18. Brené Brown, *The Power of Vulnerability: Teachings on Authenticity, Connection, and Courage* (Louisville, CO: Sounds True, 2012).

Chapter 3

1. Jerome Bruner, *The Cultural of Education* (Cambridge, MA: Harvard University Press, 1996), 46–47.
2. Deani Van Pelt and Elaine Cooper, "Treasure in the Skip: Rescue and Renewal of Charlotte Mason's Educational Vision," *Comment*, June 1, 2023, https://comment.org/treasure-in-the-skip/.
3. Susana Sendra Ramos, Pedro Lara Astiaso, and Susana Miro Lopez, "'Take Heed That Ye Offend Not—Despise Not—Hinder Not—One of These Little Ones': Charlotte Mason and Her Educational Proposal," *International Journal of Christianity and Education* 26, no. 2 (2022): 169.
4. Van Pelt and Cooper, "Treasure in the Skip."
5. Ronald Takaki, *A Different Mirror: A History of Multicultural America* (New York: Back Bay Books, 2008); Ronald Takaki, *A Different Mirror for Young People: A History of Multicultural America*, adapted by Rebecca Stefoff (New York: Triangle Square, 2012).

6. Associated Press, "Words like 'Diversity,' 'Inclusion,' to Be Removed from Georgia Teaching Program Standards," *U.S. News and World Report*, June 9, 2023, https://www.usnews.com/news/best-states/georgia/articles/2023-06-09/words-like-diversity-inclusion-to-be-removed-from-georgia-teaching-program-standards.
7. C. A. Bridges, "A Complete Look at the African American History Standards in Florida Drawing Big Criticism," *USA Today*, July 24, 2023, https://www.usatoday.com/story/news/education/2023/07/24/black-history-standards-florida/70458703007/; Francis Wilkinson, "Make America Great Again for Whom?," *Bloomberg*, August 23, 2023, https://www.bloomberg.com/opinion/articles/2023-08-23/african-american-history-bans-reflect-effort-to-whitewash-nation-s-history; Yvonne So, "Asian American History Is Already Whitewashed, and It's About to Get Even Worse," AZCentral, April 16, 2023, https://www.azcentral.com/story/opinion/op-ed/2023/04/16/asian-american-immigration-history-whitewashed-critical-race-theory-makes-worse/70115317007/.
8. Carolyn Pope Edwards, "'Fine Designs' from Italy: Montessori Education and the Reggio Approach," *Montessori Life*, Winter 2003, http://digitalcommons.unl.edu/famconfacpub/20.
9. Edwards.
10. Jack Petrash, *Understanding Waldorf Education: Teaching from the Inside Out* (Beltsville, MD: Gryphon House, 2002).
11. Petrash, 16.
12. Casey Patrick Cochran, "A Radical Ideology for Home Education: The Journey of John Holt from School Critic to Home School Advocate: 1964–1985," *Home School Researcher* 13, no. 3 (1999): 1–10.
13. Cochran, 2.
14. Cochran.
15. Patrick Farenga, "The Foundations of Unschooling," Growing Without Schooling, https://www.johnholtgws.com/writing-by-patrick/the-foundations-of-unschooling.
16. Akilah S. Richards, *Raising Free People: Unschooling as Liberation and Healing Work* (Oakland, CA: PM Press, 2020).
17. Karl Aubrey and Alison Riley, *Understanding and Using Educational Theories* (Los Angeles: Sage, 2016).
18. Michelle P. Prytula, "Teacher Metacognition Within the Professional Learning Community," *International Education Studies* 5, no. 4 (2012): 112–21.
19. Roxann Kriete and Carol Davis, *The Morning Meeting Book: K–8*, 3rd ed. (Turner Falls, MA: 2014).
20. Kriete and Davis.

Chapter 4

1. Zachary Schermele, "Teacher Shortages Continue to Plague U.S.: 86% of Public Schools Struggle to Hire Teachers," *USA Today*, October 17, 2023, https://www.usatoday.com/story/news/education/2023/10/17/teacher-shortage-2023-us-schools-struggle-hiring/71208579007/.
2. Naaz Modan, "NCES: Over Half of School Leaders Report Feeling Understaffed," K–12Dive, September 27, 2022, https://www.k12dive.com/news/nces-over-half-of-school-leaders-report-feeling-understaffed/632703/.
3. "Addressing the Teacher Shortage with American Rescue Plan Funds," US Department of Education, https://www2.ed.gov/documents/coronavirus/teacher-shortage.pdf.

4. Diane Ravitch, *The Death and Life of the Great American School System: How Testing and Choice Are Undermining Education* (New York: Basic Books, 2010).
5. Hannah Notess, "A Conversation with Diane Ravitch," *Response*, Spring 2012, https://spu.edu/depts/uc/response/new/2012-spring/features/conversation-with-diane-ravitch.asp.
6. Najarian R. Peters, "The Right to Be and Become: Black Home-Educators as Child Privacy Protectors," *Michigan Journal of Race and Law* 25, no. 1 (2020): 21–59.
7. Jonah Schenker, "Want Vibrant, Engaged Teachers? Give Them Professional Freedom," *Education Week*, November 6, 2022, https://www.edweek.org/teaching-learning/opinion-want-vibrant-engaged-teachers-give-them-professional-freedom/2022/11.
8. Jacqueline Jordan Irvine, *Black Students and School Failure: Policies, Practices, and Prescriptions* (London: Bloomsbury Academic, 1991).
9. Irvine.
10. Karl Aubrey and Alison Riley, *Understanding and Using Educational Theories* (Los Angeles: Sage, 2016).
11. Cheryl Fields-Smith, *Exploring Single Black Mothers' Resistance Through Homeschooling* (New York: Palgrave Macmillan, 2020); Jennifer Lois, *Home Is Where the School Is: The Logic of Homeschooling and the Emotional Labor of Mothering* (New York: New York University Press, 2012).
12. "Racial Disparities in ADHD," American Psychiatric Association, October 22, 2020, https://www.psychiatry.org/news-room/apa-blogs/racial-disparities-in-adhd.
13. Paul L. Morgan and Eric Hengyu Hu, "Sociodemographic Disparities in ADHD Diagnosis and Treatment Among U.S. Elementary Schoolchildren," *Psychiatry Research* 327 (2023): 115393.
14. "Racial Disparities in ADHD"; Morgan and Hu, "Sociodemographic Disparities in ADHD."
15. Rachel Aviv, "Georgia's Separate and Unequal Special-Education System," *New Yorker*, September 24, 2018, https://www.newyorker.com/magazine/2018/10/01/georgias-separate-and-unequal-special-education-system.
16. Amber M. Neal-Stanley, "'Out of the Mouths of Babes': Testimonies of Black Student Experiences in a Modern-Day Segregation Academy," *Religion and Education* 50, no. 4 (2023): 320–47.
17. Neal-Stanley, 1.
18. Neal-Stanley.
19. Edward J. Smith and Shaun R. Harper, *Disproportionate Impact of K–12 School Suspension and Expulsion on Black Students in Southern States* (Philadelphia: University of Pennsylvania, Center for the Study of Race and Equity in Education, 2015), https://race.usc.edu/wp-content/uploads/2020/08/Pub-14-Smith-and-Harper.pdf.
20. Terri J. Sabol et al., "A Window into Racial and Socioeconomic Status Disparities in Preschool Disciplinary Action Using Developmental Methodology," *Annals of the New York Academy of Sciences* 1508, no. 1 (2022): 123–36.
21. "Homeschool Laws by State," Home School Legal Defense Association, https://hslda.org/legal.
22. Bri'Anna Collins, S. Andrew Garbacz, and Tunette Powell, "Reframing Family-School Partnerships to Disrupt Disenfranchisement of Black Families and Promote Reciprocity in Collaboration," *Journal of School Psychology* 104 (2024): 101290.
23. Michael J. Dumas, "'Losing an Arm': Schooling as a Site of Black Suffering," *Race Ethnicity and Education* 17, no. 1 (2014): 1–29.

24. Alia Wong, "Enrichment Only for the Rich? How School Segregation Continues to Divide Students by Income," *USA Today*, May 16, 2024, https://www.usatoday.com/story/news/education/2024/05/16/brown-v-board-turns-70-school-segregation-persists/73243509007/.
25. Dumas, "Losing an Arm."
26. "Why Teachers Quit in 2024," Devlin Peck, January 11, 2024, https://www.devlinpeck.com/content/teacher-burnout-statistics.
27. "Why Teachers Quit."

Chapter 5

1. "The Importance of Family Engagement for Student Success," Giving Compass, https://givingcompass.org/article/karen-mapp-on-the-importance-of-family-engagement.
2. Sara Lawrence-Lightfoot, *The Essential Conversation: What Parents and Teachers Can Learn from Each Other* (New York: Ballantine Books, 2004).
3. "Preparing Educators for Equitable Family, School and Community Engagement," American Association of Colleges for Teacher Education, https://videos.aacte.org/preparing-educators-for-equitable-family-school-and-community-engagement.
4. Lawrence-Lightfoot, *Essential Conversation*, 42–75.
5. Lawrence-Lightfoot.
6. Joyce L. Epstein, "School/Family/Community Partnerships: Caring for the Children We Share," *Phi Delta Kappan* 76, no. 9 (1995): 701–12.
7. Patrick B. Forsyth, Curt M. Adams, and Wayne K. Hoy, *Collective Trust: Why Schools Can't Improve Without It* (New York: Teachers College Press, 2011).
8. Kathleen V. Hoover-Dempsey and Howard M. Sandler, "Why Do Parents Become Involved in Their Children's Education?," *Review of Educational Research* 67, no. 1 (1997): 3–42.
9. Meca Williams-Johnson and Cheryl Fields-Smith, "Homeschooling Among Black Families as a Form of Parental Involvement: A Focus on Parental Role Construction, Efficacy, and Emotions," *Educational Psychologist* 57, no. 4 (2022): 252–66.
10. Najarian R. Peters, "The Right to Be and Become: Black Home Educators as Child Privacy Protectors," *Michigan Journal of Race and Law* 25, no. 1 (2020): 21–59.
11. Michael J. Dumas, "'Losing an Arm': Schooling as a Site of Black Suffering," *Race Ethnicity and Education* 17, no. 1 (2014): 1–29.
12. Peters, "Right to Be," 43–56.
13. Billye Sankofa Waters, *We Can Speak for Ourselves: Parent Involvement and Ideologies of Black Mothers in Chicago* (Rotterdam: Sense Publishers, 2015), 3.
14. Peters, "Right to Be."
15. Williams-Johnson and Fields-Smith, "Homeschooling Among Black Families."
16. Sankofa Waters, "When and Where We Enter," 1.
17. "Black Children Are Six Times More Likely to Be Shot to Death by Police," Equal Justice Initiative, December 2, 2020, https://eji.org/news/black-children-are-six-times-more-likely-to-be-shot-to-death-by-police/.
18. Mercy Agyepong, "The Racial Achievement Gap: The Danger of a Single Story of Black Students," *Visible*, February 1, 2023, https://visiblemagazine.com/the-racial-achievement-gap-the-danger-of-a-single-story-of-black-students/.
19. Munira Z. Gunja et al., "Insights into the U.S. Maternal Mortality Crisis: An International Comparison," Commonwealth Fund, June 4, 2024, https://www.commonwealthfund.org/publications/issue-briefs/2024/jun/insights-us-maternal-mortality-crisis-international-comparison.

20. Mia Brantley, "Can't Just Send Our Children Out: Intensive Motherwork and Experiences of Black Motherhood," *Social Problems* 20 (2023): 1–19.
21. Tyrone C. Howard and Rema Reynolds, "Examining Parent Involvement in Reversing the Underachievement of African American Students in Middle-Class Schools," *Educational Foundations* 22, no. 1–2 (2008): 92.
22. Dawn Marie Dow, *Mothering While Black: Boundaries and Burdens of Middle-Class Parenthood* (Oakland: University of California Press, 2019), 28.
23. Billye Sankofa Waters, *We Can Speak for Ourselves: Parent Involvement and Ideologies of Black Mothers in Chicago* (Rotterdam: Sense, 2015).
24. Howard and Reynolds, "Examining Parent Involvement"; Latisha L. Ross et al., "Racial Identity as a Context for African American Parents' School Trust and Involvement and the Impact on Student Preparation and Persistence," *Contemporary Educational Psychology* 55 (2018): 1–11.
25. Howard and Reynolds, "Examining Parent Involvement."
26. Howard and Reynolds, 90.
27. Lois Andre-Bechely, *Could It Be Otherwise? Parents and the Inequities of Public School Choice* (London: Routledge, 2006); Howard and Reynolds, "Examining Parent Involvement."
28. Ross et al., "Racial Identity."
29. Kiara Alfonseca, "Map: The Impact of Anti-DEI Legislation," ABC News, April 5, 2024, https://abcnews.go.com/US/map-impact-anti-dei-legislation/story?id=108795967.
30. Char Adams, "After a Spate of Education Bans, Florida Churches Are Taking Black History into Their Own Hands," NBC News, February 8, 2024, https://www.nbcnews.com/news/nbcblk/florida-churches-teaching-black-history-rcna135724.
31. Cheryl Fields-Smith, *Exploring Single Black Mothers' Resistance Through Homeschooling* (New York: Palgrave Macmillan, 2020).
32. Fields-Smith.
33. Patricia Hill Collins, *Black Feminist Thought: Knowledge, Consciousness, and the Politics of Empowerment*, 2nd ed. (New York: Routledge, 2009).
34. Melissa V. Harris-Perry, *Sister Citizen: Shame, Stereotypes, and Black Women in America* (New Haven, CT: Yale University Press, 2013).
35. Harris-Perry, 28–75.
36. Robin A. Lenhardt, "Parenting While Black," *Fordham Law Review* 90, no. 6 (2022): 2592.
37. Camille Wilson Cooper, "School Choice and the Standpoint of African American Mothers: Considering the Power of Positionality," *Journal of Negro Education* 74, no. 2 (2005): 180.
38. Cooper, 181.
39. Camille Wilson Cooper, "Parent Involvement, African American Mothers, and the Politics of Educational Care," *Equity and Excellence in Education* 42, no. 4 (2009): 379–94.
40. Cooper, "Parent Involvement," 387; Camille Wilson Cooper, "The Detrimental Impact of Teacher Bias: Lessons Learned from the Standpoint of African American Mothers," *Teacher Education Quarterly* 30, no. 3 (2003): 101–16.
41. Dyan Watson, "A Message from a Black Mom to Her Son," in *Teaching for Black Lives*, ed. Dyan Watson, Jesse Hagopian, and Wayne Au (Milwaukee: Rethinking Schools, 2018), 356.
42. Watson, "Message from a Black Mom," 358.
43. Fabienne Doucet, "Parent Involvement as Ritualized Practice," *Anthropology and Education* 42, no. 4 (2011): 404–21.
44. Doucet, 404.

45. Doucet, 409.
46. Doucet, 405.
47. See Andre-Bechely, *Could It Be Otherwise?*; Annette Lareau, *Unequal Childhoods: Class, Race, and Family Life*, 2nd ed. (Oakland: University of California Press, 2011).
48. Paula Penn-Nabrit, *Morning by Morning: How We Home-Schooled Our African-American Sons to the Ivy League* (New York: Villard Books, 2003), 5.
49. Penn-Nabrit, 6.
50. Fields-Smith, *Single Black Mothers' Resistance.*
51. Ama Mazama and Garvey Musumunu, *African Americans and Homeschooling: Motivations, Opportunities, and Challenges* (New York: Routledge, 2014).
52. Ama Mazama and Garvey Lundy, "African American Homeschooling as Racial Protectionism," *Journal of Black Studies* 443, no. 7 (2012), 734.
53. Mazama and Lundy, 735.
54. Fields-Smith, *Single Black Mothers' Resistance*, 83–103.
55. See Mazama and Musumunu, *African Americans and Homeschooling*; and Ama Mazama and Garvey Lundy, "African American Homeschoolers: The Force of Faith and the Reality of Race in the Homeschooling Experience," *Religion and Education* 41, no. 3 (2014): 256–72.
56. Cheryl Fields-Smith and Timberly L. Baker, "Centering the Lived Experiences of Rural Black Homeschool Families," *Thresholds in Education* 46, no. 3 (2023): 399–419.
57. Angela Calabrese Barton et al., "Ecologies of Parental Engagement in Urban Education," *Educational Researcher* 33, no. 4 (2004): 3–12.
58. Edward M. Olivos, *The Power of Parents: A Critical Perspective of Bicultural Parent Involvement in Public Schools* (New York: Peter Lang, 2006).
59. Aixa D. Marchand et al., "Integrating Race, Racism, and Critical Consciousness in Black Parents' Engagement with Schools," *Journal of Family Theory and Review* 11 (2019): 367–84.
60. Marchand et al., 370–71.
61. Cynthia B. Dillard, *On Spiritual Strivings: Transforming an African American Woman's Academic Life* (New York: State University of New York Press, 2006); Cynthia B. Dillard, *The Spirit of Our Work: Black Women Teachers (Re)member* (Boston: Beacon, 2022).
62. Vanessa Siddle Walker, *Their Highest Potential: An African American School Community in the Segregated South* (Chapel Hill: University of North Carolina Press, 1996); James D. Anderson, *Education of Blacks in the South: 1860–1935* (Chapel Hill: University of North Carolina Press, 1988).
63. Walker, *Their Highest Potential*; Collins, *Black Feminist Thought.*
64. Latoya Sherrica Johnson, "Using Sista Circles to Examine the Professional Experience of Contemporary Black Women Teachers in Schools: A Collective Story About School Culture and Support" (PhD diss., University of Georgia, 2015).
65. Thank you, Cynthia B. Dillard and the What Does Ghana Have to Teach Us Study Abroad Program.
66. Carla Patrice Wellborn and Timberly L. Baker, "BlackWashing: How Black Home Education is (Mis)represented in Quantitative Homeschooling Literature," in *Toward a Freedom Praxis: The Enduring Significance of Black Home Education*, ed. Cheryl Fields-Smith, T. Elon Dancy, and Martez Files, special issue, *Negro Educational Review*, forthcoming.
67. Elise Trumbull et al., *Bridging Cultures Between Home and School: A Guide for Teachers* (Northfleet, UK: WestEd, 2001).
68. Howard and Reynolds, "Examining Parent Involvement."

69. Karen Hale Hankins, *Teaching Through the Storm: A Journal of Hope* (New York: Teachers College Press, 2003).
70. Hankins, 2.
71. Laura S. Abrams and Jewelle Taylor Gibbs, "Disrupting the Logic of Home-School Relations: Parent Involvement Strategies and Practices of Inclusion and Exclusion," *Urban Education* 37, no. 3 (2002): 404.
72. Kristine S. Lewis Grant et al., "Bridging Multilingual Families and Schools: Cultural Brokering as Social Justice Leadership Practice," *Journal of Family Diversity in Education* 5, no. 1 (2022): 37–58.
73. Grant et al.
74. Tiffanie Turner-Henderson and Maureen Leary, "Fictive Kinship Networks in Postsecondary Education: Lessons Learned from the 'Village,'" in *Multifaceted Strategies for Social-Emotional Learning and Whole Learner Education*, ed. Carissa McCray (Hershey, PA: IGI Global, 2021), 64–85.
75. Robert Taylor et al., "Fictive Kin Networks Among African Americans, Black Caribbeans, and Non-Latino Whites," *Journal of Family Issues* 43, no. 1 (2021): 20–46.
76. Shakhnoza Kayumova et al., "Latina Mothers and Daughters: Ways of Knowing, Being, and Becoming in the Context of Bilingual Family Science Workshops," *Anthropology and Education Quarterly* 46, no. 3 (2015): 260–76.

Chapter 6

1. Michael Battle, *Ubuntu: I in You and You in Me* (New York: Seabury Books, 2009), 1–27.
2. Battle, 3–7.
3. Quoted in Battle, 2.
4. Renee Tougas, "Resisting and Disrupting Neoliberal Subjectivity in Self-Directed Education: What Can We Learn from Black Homeschoolers," *On the Horizon*, published ahead of print, July 2, 2024, https://doi.org/10.1108/OTH-03-2024-0010.
5. Tougas, 11.
6. Vanessa Siddle Walker, *Their Highest Potential: An African American School Community in the Segregated South* (Chapel Hill: University of North Carolina Press, 1996).
7. Angela Calabrese Barton et al., "Ecologies of Parental Engagement in Urban Education," *Educational Researcher* 33, no. 4 (2004): 3–12.
8. Cheryl Fields-Smith and Meca Williams, "Motivations, Sacrifices, and Challenges: Black Parents' Decisions to Home School," *Urban Review* 41, no. 4 (2009): 369–89.
9. Aaron Hirsh, *The Changing Landscape of Homeschooling in the United States* (Center on Reinventing Public Education, 2019), https://files.eric.ed.gov/fulltext/ED596627.pdf.
10. Hirsh, 1.
11. Hirsh, 1.
12. Hirsh, 5.
13. Vicki Caruana, "Partnering with Homeschoolers," Association for Supervision and Curriculum Development, September 1, 1999, https://ascd.org/el/articles/partnering-with-homeschoolers.
14. Caruana.
15. Caruana.
16. Libby Stanford and Mark Lieberman, "Education Savings Accounts Explained," *Education Week*, April 26, 2023, https://www.edweek.org/policy-politics/education-savings-accounts-explained/2023/03.

17. "Education Quality Basic Education Act: Enacted," *Georgia State University Law Review* 1, no. 2 (1985): 307, https://readingroom.law.gsu.edu/cgi/viewcontent.cgi?article=2569&context=gsulr.
18. Cheryl Fields-Smith, *Exploring Single Black Mothers' Resistance Through Homeschooling* (New York: Palgrave Macmillan, 2020).

Acknowledgments

First and foremost, I am deeply grateful to God, from whom all things are made possible (Matthew 19:26). Your grace and guidance created this opportunity and sustained me throughout the writing journey.

I extend my heartfelt appreciation to Molly Cerrone, Michael Higgins, and the other members of the Harvard Education Press team, whose unwavering encouragement and insightful feedback enriched this book beyond measure.

To Najarian Peters, whose brilliant research on Black home educators as privacy protectors undergirds this text, thank you for your tremendous contribution to the literature on Black homeschooling. Thank you also for being a wonderful colleague and friend. You inspire me.

Special thanks to my Thursday Gwinnett Writing Buddies, Kiana Willis and Brittany Kilgore, for your thoughtful discussions, inspiration, and joy.

To my writing sisters, Gayle Andrews, Kyunghwa Lee, and Dorothy White: your camaraderie, constructive critiques, and shared experiences have been a constant source of inspiration.

Thank you to my Harambee Scholars for keeping me uplifted and pushing me to strive for clarity and excellence in my work.

I am indebted to the Spencer Foundation for its generous support through the 2006 Small Research Grant, which provided the essential resources for the initial exploration of Black home education that underpins this book.

This research has also been aided by the generous support of the Center for Educational Opportunity at Albany State University. Thank you for your encouragement and support.

Lastly, to all those whose names may not appear here but whose contributions, whether big or small, have led to the realization of this project, I am truly thankful.

Thank you all for believing in this work and for being a part of this transformative journey.

With profound gratitude,

Cheryl Fields-Smith

About the Author

Cheryl Fields-Smith is a professor of elementary education in the Department of Educational Theory and Practice (ETAP) at the University of Georgia's Mary Frances Early College of Education in Athens, Georgia. She has been a member of the ETAP faculty for twenty years and currently serves as ETAP's associate department head, after serving as the graduate program coordinator for three years. Fields-Smith earned her doctoral degree from Emory University in 2004 under the direction of Vanessa Siddle Walker. She is a former elementary school teacher who taught first, second, and fourth grades in her home state of Connecticut.

Fields-Smith's research interests center on understanding Black parents' engagement in their children's education from the perspective of Black parents. She is a pioneer in Black homeschool research, having published the first empirically based study in 2009 with the article "Motivations, Sacrifices, and Challenges: Black Parents' Decisions to Home School," coauthored with a doctoral student who served as her research assistant on a Spencer Foundation grant at the time. Since this publication, Fields-Smith has written a book titled *Exploring Single Black Mothers' Resistance Through Homeschooling*, coedited a book titled *Homeschooling Black Children in the U.S.: Theory, Practice, and Popular Culture*, and published several articles and chapters on Black home education. Her work has been featured on major networks and other multimedia broadcasts.

Index